THE BARBARIANS

LOST CIVILIZATIONS

The books in this series explore the rise and fall of the great civilizations and peoples of the ancient world. Each book considers not only their history but their art, culture and lasting legacy and asks why they remain important and relevant in our world today.

Already published:

The Barbarians Peter Bogucki
Egypt Christina Riggs
The Indus Andrew Robinson
The Persians Geoffrey Parker and Brenda Parker

THE
BARBARIANS

LOST CIVILIZATIONS

PETER BOGUCKI

REAKTION BOOKS

To Jim Wei and Vince Poor, for the opportunity to pursue my scholarship and their collegial interest in my work

Published by Reaktion Books Ltd
Unit 32, Waterside
44–48 Wharf Road
London N1 7UX, UK

www.reaktionbooks.co.uk

First published 2017
Copyright © Peter Bogucki 2017

Printed and bound in China

A catalogue record for this book is available from the British Library

ISBN 978 1 78023 718 3

CONTENTS

CHRONOLOGY

c. 9500 BC	Establishment of relatively modern vegetation and wildlife in temperate Europe
c. 7000 BC	Domestic plants and animals appear in Greece
c. 5500 BC	Expansion of farming begins in central Europe
c. 4000 BC	Adoption of farming by hunter-gatherers in southern Scandinavia and British Isles; first 'lake-dwelling' settlements built in Alpine Foreland
c. 4000–3500 BC	Wheeled vehicles are invented, probably in central or southeast Europe
3384–3370 BC	Arbon-Bleiche 3 on Lake Constance inhabited
c. 3300 BC	Ötzi the Iceman is killed crossing the Alps
c. 3200 BC	Passage grave at Newgrange is built in Ireland
c. 2900 BC	Construction of first bank and ditch begins at Stonehenge

c. 2620–2480 BC	Stonehenge is expanded to full extent
c. 2400–2300 BC	Amesbury Archer dies near Stonehenge
c. 2500–2000 BC	Transition from Stone Age to Bronze Age in temperate Europe
2049 BC	Seahenge is built on English coast
c. 2000 BC	Man in Bush Barrow near Stonehenge buried with lavish grave goods
c. 1550 BC	Dover Boat abandoned
c. 1370 BC	Egtved Girl is buried in an oak coffin in Denmark
1365–967 BC	Flag Fen ritual platform is built and maintained in eastern England
c. 1000–800 BC	Transition from Bronze Age to Iron Age in temperate Europe
c. 800–500 BC	Intensive salt mining at Hallstatt
747–722 BC	Biskupin built in northern Poland
c. 600 BC	Greeks establish trading colony at Massalia, southern France
c. 590–530 BC	Mud-brick wall in use at Heuneburg, southwestern Germany

c. 400 BC–AD 400	Bog bodies are deposited in wetlands across northern Europe
c. 350–300 BC	Hjortspring Boat is deposited in bog with weapons sacrifice
c. 300 BC	La Tène art style appears in western Europe
c. 200 BC–AD 400	'Royal' sites in Ireland flourish
148 BC	Corlea Trackway built in Ireland
58 BC	Caesar invades Gaul
AD 9	Slaughter of Varus' legions in Teutoberg Forest by native forces led by Arminius
AD 43	Romans invade Britain
c. AD 200	War-booty sacrifice made at Illerup Ådal A
AD 310–20	Nydam Boat constructed in northern Germany
AD 406	Barbarians cross the Rhine in force, devastation ensues
AD 410	Goths sack Rome, Roman officials leave Britain
AD 451	Romans and Visigoths defeat Huns at Châlons, eastern France
AD 476	Conventional date for final collapse of Roman Empire in the West

AD 480	Sandby Borg on island of Öland sacked, inhabitants massacred
AD 481/2	Childeric, king of the Franks, is buried in Tournai, Belgium
AD 496	Childeric's son Clovis converts to Christianity
AD 1557	Concept of a 'Migration Period' introduced by Wolfgang Lazius for population movements during the first millennium AD
AD 1808	William Cunnington excavates Bush Barrow near Stonehenge
AD 1854	Ferdinand Keller investigates Swiss lake-dwelling sites
AD 1933	Walenty Szwajcer discovers Biskupin in Poland
AD 1950	Tollund Man discovered in Denmark
AD 1987	Tony Clunn finds the site of an important Roman defeat in the Teutoberg Forest
AD 1991	Ötzi the Iceman found by hikers in the Alps
AD 2014	New Iron Age 'royal tomb' is discovered at Lavau in France

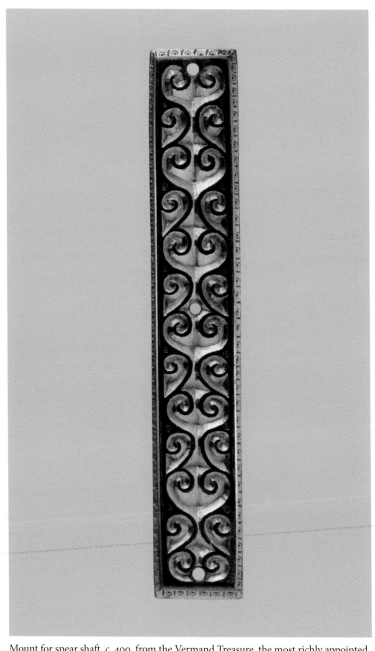

Mount for spear shaft, *c.* 400, from the Vermand Treasure, the most richly appointed barbarian warrior grave ever found. The grave was likely that of an auxiliary soldier stationed in the Roman province of Gaul.

PREFACE

The civilizations of Greece and Rome that flourished in Mediterranean Europe did not develop in isolation. To their north, non-literate peoples inhabited river valleys, mountains, plains and coasts from the Atlantic to the Urals. The ancient Mediterranean civilizations called them 'barbarians' as a way of marking them as different and alien. Their story, known almost exclusively through archaeological finds of settlements, offerings, monuments and burials, is as compelling as that of the great literate, urban civilizations. Moreover, the prehistoric past of Europe echoes into the modern era through new discoveries, celebrations of the past, tourist attractions and even politics.

Classical civilizations on the north shore of the Mediterranean Sea were surrounded by barbarians in Europe, southwest Asia and North Africa. This book deals with the barbarians that lived in Europe, the area where my archaeological research has been concentrated. Unlike most discussions of barbarians that pick up when these peoples made contact with classical civilizations, I will show that the societies that met the Greeks and Romans in the final millennium BC had a long prehistoric heritage. As an archaeologist, I privilege the material record over written accounts, and one of the aims of this book is to show the reader what archaeology can tell us that texts cannot.

Let me acknowledge that the title *The Barbarians: Lost Civilizations* is an oxymoron. By definition, the people we call barbarians were not civilized, in terms of what the concept of 'civilization' meant to the inhabitants of Greece and Rome. Except for those few who were schooled in neighbouring literate societies, European barbarians did not write or speak Greek or Latin. With the exception of the large towns known as *oppida* at the end of the first millennium BC, they did not live in settlements that might be called urban. The organizing principles of their communities were chaotic in comparison with the hierarchies and rules that structured Greek and Roman society. They fail just about every test of what it means to be 'civilized'.

When viewed over the long arc of time that begins in the Stone Age, however, the European barbarians reveal a remarkable story of innovation, mobility and social complexity. They traded, farmed, herded and fought with energy and enthusiasm. Some members of barbarian society sought status, wealth and prestige, while others went about their everyday work. When they encountered civilizations, they cunningly took advantage of new opportunities for social mobility. Just because barbarians were different from Greeks and Romans does not mean that they are any less interesting.

This book should not be taken as a definitive grand narrative of the European barbarians. Instead, it hits the highlights as I see them, especially of topics that I personally have found interesting over the last forty years of archaeological research, teaching and writing. I hope that the reader will find many of these intriguing and will seek further information. Much is available on the Internet, although this information has to be regarded critically. More can be learned by visiting sites and museums across barbarian Europe that exhibit, interpret and reconstruct the material world of these prehistoric societies.

The legacy of the Barbarian World remains with us today. Thus another goal of this book is to bring the barbarian story into the present day and reflect on how we have come to view the pre-literate peoples of Europe. The final chapter talks about the role of the barbarian narrative in modern history, politics and culture.

INTRODUCTION

Between 2000 BC and AD 500,[1] Europe north of the Alps was inhabited by remarkable societies that matched the classical civilizations of the Mediterranean in many respects except one: literacy. They remain relatively invisible in the historical narrative of the emergence of European society except to be grouped under the single name of 'barbarians'. We know a tremendous amount about these peoples, and the privileging of written sources from classical authors simply overlooks the rich body of evidence about them. Their monuments are visible across the European landscape, while beneath the surface lie their settlements and their graves. Yet they come across in the popular imagination as violent, bloodthirsty killers responsible for the collapse of Rome and other crimes against humanity.

This book attempts to redress this traditional indictment of barbarians. Lest the reader think that it will be 'Springtime for Arminius,'[2] let me stress that there will be no effort here to make the prehistoric inhabitants of northern Europe appear more civilized than they were. Their bad reputation has been amplified over the centuries, which also allows them to be dismissed from history. Yet we really should care who built Stonehenge, what it means to make bronze and iron, and above all, who were the people that the Greeks and Romans met when they went north.

Since we do not know the names of people who lived in northern areas until very late in the story, we have to understand them as communities linked by similar things and practices as well as deep pasts. We do not know how they thought of their own identities, but we can be sure that they never considered themselves to be barbarians. They were farmers, traders, metalsmiths, chiefs, slaves, parents and children just like everyone else. Collectively, they made up what I will call 'the Barbarian World'.

The Barbarian World was not a monolithic entity. Over the 3,000 years that are the focus of this book, it was transformed many times. It also varied geographically, from Ireland to Russia and from the Arctic Circle to the Alps. Yet throughout this area, ancient people had contacts across great distances and passed down traditions and memories across the centuries. The fact that barbarians could not write does not mean that they should be written out of history.

The problem with written sources

It is true that classical authors did write about the barbarians, and myths and sagas that were not recorded until later can be projected backward into the pre-literate past. Many classical authors who wrote about the barbarians never actually met one, however, and extrapolation from indirect sources produces a confused mixture of legends and details. Ethnohistoric narratives and travellers' accounts from later centuries are better sources, but they have limited coverage and provide only snapshots of complex social, political and religious arrangements.

The most important problem with written sources about non-literate peoples is that they impose the viewpoint of the writer. This is always a problem for historians. As Winston Churchill said about Stanley Baldwin, 'history will say that the right honourable gentleman was wrong . . . because I shall write the history.'[3] Luckily other people also wrote about British politics in the 1930s, so historians can evaluate whether Churchill's account is accurate. With non-literate ancient peoples, writing by superordinated literate authors imposes a particular perspective. For example, almost all accounts of the life of African slaves in the Antebellum South were written by white authors, for it was illegal to teach the slaves how to write (although some did learn to do so). Thus, our knowledge of their everyday lives is either unrecorded or badly skewed.

The same constraint applies in prehistoric Europe. Accounts by Greek and Roman chroniclers were not written impartially, nor were they intended for an impartial readership. As we will see below, it suited Caesar and other Roman writers to establish a sharp distinction between the pacified peoples living within the Imperial frontiers and the unpacified peoples living outside. Such a distinction may or may not have been real, and there are indications that this differentiation does not reflect the inherent social and ethnic similarities across the frontier. Thus the relatively few written sources about the Barbarian World that we have from classical authors must be taken not as definitive but simply as one line of evidence, and a flawed one at that.

Archaeology as a primary source

Direct knowledge of the Barbarian World comes almost completely from archaeology, the study of the material remains of past peoples from which we can infer details of their lives and practices. Several centuries of archaeological study of the last several millennia BC and the first millennium AD have yielded a huge body of information that fills museums and archaeological laboratories across Europe. Archaeologists populate universities, museum staffs, national and regional antiquities offices and private firms that engage in rescue archaeology. Scholars from North America and as far away as Japan have been involved in the study of European archaeology. On the basis of the archaeology, there is a lot that can be said about the Barbarian World, but there is so much more that we still do not know.

Archaeology in northern and central Europe involves the study of ancient sites and the artefacts that they contain, as well as stray finds recovered from rivers, sea floors, glaciers and other unusual places. It differs from archaeology of the classical world of Greece and Rome and the civilizations of Egypt and the Near East in that European sites are rather mundane by comparison. There is no Acropolis, no Pyramids of Giza, no Colosseum. With a few imported exceptions, the sites left by the barbarians do not have inscriptions or texts. Figurative sculpture is largely absent, unless acquired by trade. An archaeologist looks at an immense hillfort like Maiden Castle in southern England with awe, but to the uninitiated it looks like a lot of ditches around a hill. Even Stonehenge, whose photographs make it appear huge, is puny by comparison with major classical monuments.

Instead, the sites of barbarian Europe are small, often invisible on the surface. The most evident are thousands of burial mounds, also known as tumuli or barrows. They are almost everywhere, and many more have been destroyed over the intervening millennia. Other graves lie buried in cemeteries or individual tombs. Mortuary sites of the barbarians have often yielded spectacular grave offerings. Human bodies are also found in unusual places, mummified high in the Alps or submerged in bogs, often having met grisly deaths.

Evidence for prehistoric settlement is everywhere in Europe, ranging from the earliest hunters of the Ice Age, through the earliest farmers, herders and metalworkers, until the dawn of literate civilization. Most settlements cannot be seen, since timber was the main building material, and wood decays unless waterlogged. Thus much of what we know about ancient buildings in Europe

Stone Age longhouse at Łoniowa, Poland, being excavated, showing postholes and pits.

comes from stains in the soil where upright timbers were set into postholes and trenches. The variety of structures is astonishing: long, short, round, oval, rectangular, big, small. Although we know a lot about their outlines, we know less about the structures and roofs, although we can make educated guesses.

In and around the houses, ancient people dug pits. Sometimes the pits were to provide clay for plastering the walls. Others were used for storage. After serving their original purpose, pits usually were receptacles for rubbish. Archaeologists love rubbish. It contains broken pottery, which shows regional differences, changes over time and affinities with other sites. Worn-out tools and manufacturing waste tell us about ancient technology and material use. Animal bones and charred seeds enable reconstruction of the ancient diet. Waterlogged deposits contain pollen, insects and plant remains that give a broad picture of life in the settlement. A full rubbish pit can tell many tales that cannot be found in written sources.

Finally, there are ritual sites, of which Stonehenge is the most celebrated example. Some stand out in the landscape, like stone circles, while others are hidden. The Hjortspring Boat in Denmark contained the weapons, shields and tools of a defeated invading army sacrificed in thanks by the victors. Rock carvings are abundant across Scandinavia and in the Alps. Bogs and other wet places had special spiritual significance, as did now-invisible groves of trees.

For all this wealth of information, sites and artefacts by themselves tell us very little without the analytical techniques applied to them. Pottery and tools can be grouped by form and decoration to show similarities and differences among sites. Archaeobotanists and zooarchaeologists study seeds and animal bones. Chemists find residues of animal fats from meat and milk in pottery. Burials yield ancient DNA preserved in the teeth and bones. Strontium isotope ratios from teeth can tell whether someone grew up locally or elsewhere, which gives information about movement, sometimes over surprising distances. Computers permit the study of vast quantities of information and enable visualization of artefacts, houses and settlements.

Many people compare archaeology to a vast jigsaw puzzle. An archaeologist often responds, yes, it might be like a jigsaw puzzle, but someone has thrown away 90 per cent of the pieces, and there's no picture on the box. A more apt analogy is trying to figure out what is in a room by looking through the keyhole, although nowadays old-fashioned keyholes are no longer found. New discoveries cause old conclusions to be questioned. Archaeologists often disagree over how ancient societies should be reconstructed, and thus nothing that we think we now know about the Barbarian World should be taken as set in stone for eternity.

Telling time

For archaeology to work, we need to know how old things are. There are two types of archaeological time: relative and absolute. Since a fundamental principle of archaeology is that older things are buried beneath newer things, we can establish relationships in time between two types of remains by finding circumstances in which one is buried beneath another. Thus relative time can be established only when objects are found lying in the places and layers where ancient people left them. Laborious compilation of these sequences by archaeologists over the last two centuries provides a good idea of the relative age of just about anything found on ancient sites in Europe.

Absolute dates, which situate finds in calendrical years but really are not as precise as non-archaeologists might think, require scientific methods. When wood is preserved due to waterlogging or desiccation, the study of the tree rings by comparison to standard regional sequences of thickness that result from annual variations in rainfall can yield dates to the year or the season. Carbon-14 dating, also called radiocarbon dating, was developed after the Second World War and is based on the decay of the radioactive isotope of carbon, carbon-14, to nitrogen-14. Recent improvements in this method have led to greater precision, permitting dates to be established within a half-century. For the study of the Barbarian World, these two methods are the primary techniques to establish the calendrical age of sites and artefacts.

C. J. Thomsen, painted in 1848 by Johan Vilhelm Gertner.

Once the age of sites and artefacts has been established, we fit them into broader systems of relationships. In the study of ancient Europe, the basic structure for discussing larger patterns is called the Three-age System.[4] Two centuries after it was devised, it continues in use for the overall division of time in ancient Europe. Today, archaeologists use the terms Stone Age, Bronze Age and Iron Age as a shorthand for facilitating conversations.

In 1816, Christian Jurgensen Thomsen (1788–1865) was appointed curator of the Danish National Museum. The collections were a chaotic mess, and Thomsen needed to figure out how to display them sensibly. He had the clever idea of sorting tools according to the materials from which they were made: stone, bronze and iron. Thomsen extended his classification to other objects that were found with the implements. For example, he noted that certain pottery types were found only with stone tools, while glass beads only occurred with iron tools. Thomsen's assistant, Jens Jacob Asmusssen Worsaae (1821–1885), took the Three-age System from museum displays to field excavations. This required careful observation of the relationships between types of finds to establish their relative dating. Such attention to the context of finds established field archaeology as a professional scholarly discipline. Today, the Three-age System of Thomsen and Worsaae continues in use as the overall organizing principle of prehistoric Europe. Boundaries between the stages have been blurred, and they do not have the same absolute dates everywhere in Europe, so the reader should not assume that this system is sacrosanct. More importantly, it is crucial to understand that it is a system imposed by archaeologists. Ancient people had no idea whether they were living in the Stone, Bronze or Iron Age, and they did not wake up one morning and realize that they had gone from one to the next. While this might be a trivial point, I will try throughout this book to differentiate between what was a reality for an inhabitant of the Barbarian World and what is an interpretation imposed by archaeologists. An archaeological concept such as the Bronze Age is not only a span of time but also a set of technological, social, economic and ritual practices with roots in earlier millennia that formed the foundation for what came later.

The geography of the Barbarian World

Over sixty years ago, the British prehistorian Grahame Clark (1907–1995) recognized two broad divisions of Europe reflected in the archaeological record.[5] He called them 'Mediterranean' and 'Temperate' Europe. Mediterranean Europe consists of lands bordering that body of water and extending west to include Spain and Portugal. Its natural vegetation consists of Mediterranean evergreen forest, the result of summer drought and winter rains. In this zone, the great civilizations of Greece and Rome arose from their local precursors.

Temperate Europe is the region whose natural vegetation, before its transformation by farming and industry, was covered by deciduous forest. It reaches from the Atlantic coast and the British Isles, across central Europe and southern Scandinavia, into European Russia. Seasonal differences in this zone are sharper, as are variations in terrain. The Alps provide the highest relief, followed by the Carpathians in the east and the Scandinavian mountains in the north. Immense flatlands such as the Pannonian Plain and the North European Plain permitted easy movement, as did major river arteries such as the Danube, Elbe and Rhine. Between the North European Plain and the Alps is a zone of rolling uplands and hills, as are also found in the British Isles.

Across this landscape, people distributed themselves in different ways. Their attachment to particular regions led to distinctive forms of pottery, tools, weapons and ornaments that vary from one area to another. Moreover, these styles changed over time. After the breakthrough of the Three-age System, archaeologists in the nineteenth century soon realized that these geographical stylistic differences were key to reading the pre-literate record across Europe. The Swedish archaeologist Oscar Montelius (1843–1921) worked out the mapping of bronze artefact types in northern Europe, while the German archaeologist Paul Reinecke (1872–1958) established the chronological framework for the first millennium BC in central Europe. Other archaeologists developed the study of the interplay between geography and stylistic variation further, including the nationalistic German archaeologist Gustav Kossinna (1858–1931) and the celebrated Australian-British prehistorian V. Gordon Childe (1892–1957).

Geography plays another role in the study of the Barbarian World, namely the interaction between people and their environment. Climate change has always been a part of the human experience, and the Barbarian World experienced episodes of relative warmth and relative cold. Rainfall differed from one year to the next. Such variability had an impact on important matters such as agricultural production, and people needed to adjust to different conditions. Raw materials are also not uniformly distributed. Flint, salt, copper, tin, amber and gold are found in specific places, and thus their procurement and distribution had to take into account both their extraction and their transport to places where they were desired. Finally, people had an impact on their environment, usually for the worse. The area of western Ireland known as the Burren is a stark limestone landscape today, but before clearance and grazing during the last several centuries BC, its thin soil supported grass and trees. The use of wood for building and burning and the grazing of livestock that prevented forest regeneration dramatically changed the natural environment of Europe well before the industrial era.

Luminous regions and ordinary people

The story of the Barbarian World revolves around particular regions, which appear over and over as locations for important developments and landmark sites. We can refer to these as the 'luminous regions' of European prehistory.[6] They are usually clusters of important monumental sites, rich burials and unusual concentrations of finds. Luminous regions tend to have abundant resources like fertile soil, or they were situated at the intersection of important trade routes. Archaeologists are drawn to them because there is always something to be found, and it is likely that it will be as remarkable as previous discoveries.

In the Barbarian World, a luminous region might be an entire country, like Denmark or Ireland, whose archaeological record by itself comprises a textbook of prehistory. Sometimes, it could be a smaller region that attracted prehistoric settlement or monument building. In the British Isles, the Orkney Islands or the central part of southern Britain around Salisbury Plain – the ancient kingdom of Wessex – are such places, while in Poland, we might consider regions like Małopolska or Kuyavia to be luminous. Sometimes a luminous region is specific to a particular period, such as the watersheds of the upper Danube, Rhine, Seine and Rhône during the middle of the first millennium BC, after which it glows a bit less brightly in comparison with neighbouring areas.

This book will devote considerable attention to some of the luminous regions, because their sites and finds are a good way to tell the story of the Barbarian World. There is a temptation, however, to treat these areas as having undue significance, and it is important to remember that outside of them people also lived, prospered and struggled. Whether or not they built spectacular monuments or buried their dead in lavish tombs, ordinary people whose names we do not know made the choices and did the work that made the

Northern part of the Barbarian World with locations of sites mentioned in the text.

Barbarian World possible, whether they lived a kilometre or two from Stonehenge or in some remote Carpathian valley.

Organization and themes

The goal of this book is to provide a very high-level overview of the Barbarian World by taking advantage of the ability of archaeology to explore time and space more broadly than most historical accounts. It could be expanded considerably, and the Bibliography provides pointers towards very good books and journals that go into greater depth. At the end, the reader should appreciate the heterogeneity of the Barbarian World. Unlike the impression given by many historical accounts that report contact with pre-literate peoples at a specific time and place, there was no uniform 'barbarian culture'.

Instead, this book can be considered to be a tour of the Barbarian World. As with any itinerary, the traveller chooses places to visit selectively to obtain a representative impression of things and practices found in an area. It is impossible to be absolutely comprehensive. Instead, the hope is that the reader will get the general picture and wish to return to the Barbarian World again and again.

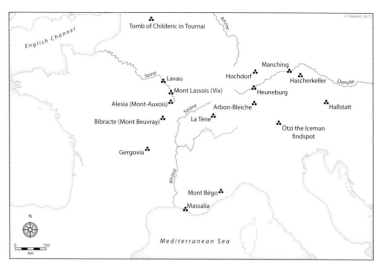

Southern part of the Barbarian World with locations of sites mentioned in the text.

The tour will proceed along a straightforward chronological track, starting in the Stone Age after the retreat of the ice sheets and ending with the establishment of literate polities across northern and western Europe. Archaeology is explicitly comparative, so regional differences will be highlighted. Case studies of particular sites and areas will illuminate broad themes, with an admitted bias towards the topics that I find interesting and sites that I have visited or studied in depth.

Let me encourage the reader to be on the lookout for major themes in the study of the ancient peoples north of the Alps. They include the following: *innovation and expertise*: the mastery of materials including wood, flint, stone, bone, antler, pigments, copper, bronze, iron, silver and gold; *connectedness*: the emergence of long-distance travel as far back as the Stone Age, as indicated by evidence for watercraft, seafaring, wheeled vehicles, trade in materials such as copper, tin, salt, luxury goods and wine, and finally evidence from isotopic analysis of human movement; *enclosure*: the practice of demarcating areas by ditches, banks, ramparts and palisades, to provide separation, protection, control or boundaries; *monumentality*: the construction of large structures that inscribed the landscape and sent a powerful message to all who saw them, as reflected in megalithic tombs, standing stones, barrows and cairns, ship burials, stone circles, hillforts, *oppida* and large and unusual buildings; *ritual*: the practice of commemorating and ceremonializing values and beliefs, which appears repeatedly in the form of elaborate burials, offerings in bogs and rivers, feasts, pilgrimages and rock art; *wealth*: the accumulation of material goods to demonstrate status and power among societal elites, which we see repeatedly in spectacular burials containing luxury goods and differentiation in architecture, eventually leading to political power in the form of chiefs and kings; and *ordinary lives*: the people who lived in farmsteads, kept livestock, tilled and harvested crops, made everyday goods, were victims of violence and disease and formed the core of the societies that populated the Barbarian World.

ONE

HUNTERS, FISHERS, FARMERS AND METALWORKERS

To begin to describe the Barbarian World, we need to pick a starting point in the European portion of the grand narrative of the human experience. This point will be arbitrary, and it could have been just as valid to start millennia earlier or centuries later. For now, however, we begin the story on Salisbury Plain in southern England around 2300 BC. During the third millenium BC, people were converging in this region, which later took the historical name of Wessex, to experience a remarkable ceremonial landscape, of which Stonehenge is but one element. We have come to know some of the people who lived there through their skeletons and the offerings buried with them. Archaeologists call one of them the 'Amesbury Archer', and we begin the Barbarian story with him.

The Archer's story

In 2002, archaeologists conducting a routine investigation where a school was planned at Amesbury in southern England, about 5 kilometres (3 mi.) south of Stonehenge, found the grave of an adult male surrounded by artefacts, lying on its left side with the head pointed northeast.[1] By the skeleton were sixteen triangular arrowheads and two wrist-guards, flat pieces of stone tied to the wrist to protect it from a bowstring. This is typical archery equipment of this period, and thus the man became known as the Amesbury Archer. In addition to arrowheads and wrist-guards, lying beside his skeleton were three copper knives, five ceramic

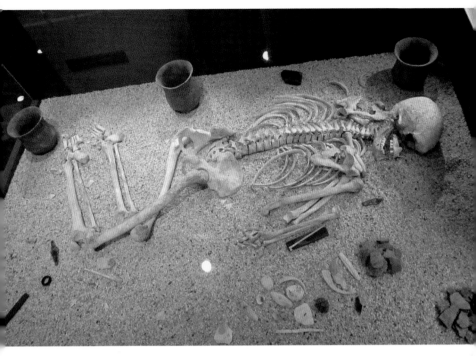

Reconstruction of the burial of the Amesbury Archer, in the Salisbury Museum.

vessels, four boars' tusks and two enigmatic gold ornaments thought to be hair or ear decorations.

The Archer's bones and teeth were full of information. His skeleton lay in a crouched position. He was between 35 and 45 years old and stood about 1.75 metres (5 ft 9 in.) tall. A knee injury earlier in life crippled him until his death. Carbon-14 dating of the Archer's bones indicated he died between 2400 and 2300 BC.

Oxygen and strontium isotopes in the Archer's teeth provided information about where he grew up. Tooth enamel forms in childhood and takes in oxygen and strontium from food and drinking water. The ratio of oxygen-18 to oxygen-16 is higher in warmer climates than in colder climates. Strontium isotope ratios are derived from the local geological structure, and the ratio of strontium-87 to strontium-86 differs geographically.[2] Together, oxygen and strontium isotope ratios record where an individual spent his or her childhood. The isotopic evidence indicates that the Archer spent his childhood and perhaps teenage years in central

Europe, probably in the foothills of the Alps in southern Germany or Switzerland, because the oxygen isotopes indicate an area colder than England, but the strontium isotopes exclude most northern areas. Although we have an idea where his tooth enamel formed, and thus probably where he was born, we do not know the route the Archer took to reach England or how long he lived there before he died.

Archaeologists call the ceramic vessels in the Archer's grave 'Bell Beakers', which were found throughout central and western Europe during the final centuries of the third millennium BC. Bell Beakers are highly decorated, handle-less drinking cups that resemble an upturned bell. They are typically found in graves like that of the Archer: a single, crouched male with arrowheads, wrist-guards and often copper tools and gold ornaments. Interestingly, the copper in the Archer's knives came from western France or northern Spain, consistent with the distribution of Bell Beakers in Atlantic Europe.

Soon after the discovery of the Archer, the skeleton of a young man about 20–25 years old was found nearby. His bones yielded a date of 2350–2260 BC. Grave goods included boars' tusks, flint tools and gold ornaments like those of the Archer, but no beaker. Both men must have been related, since they shared a rare heredi-tary fusion of foot bones, so the younger man has been called the 'Archer's Companion'. Strontium isotope ratios showed, however, that the younger man grew up locally in southern England. Was he a descendant of the Archer?

Then, archaeologists found a collective burial at Boscombe Down, also near Stonehenge, that contained the skeletons of at least five adult men, a teenager who was also probably male, and one, possibly two, children. One man was between 30 and 45 years old and had suffered an injury earlier in life that shattered his thighbone. He was buried in a crouched position with his head towards the north. The other men died in their late twenties, while the teenager was between fifteen and eighteen years old. Their dis-connected bones were spread around the skeleton of the older man, so this was not their first burial spot. All the men and the teenager seem to have been related due to shared features of their skulls.

An abundance of arrowheads in the grave led archaeologists to name these individuals the 'Boscombe Bowmen'. The beakers that accompanied them were decorated with cord impressions showing continental connections. Strontium and the oxygen ratios in their teeth narrowed their points of origin to Wales, although Brittany, Portugal, the Massif Central of France and the Black Forest are also possible. Their premolars and molars, however, had different isotopic signatures, indicating that the Bowmen lived in one place until the ages of five to seven and another between the ages of eleven and thirteen, before moving to the Stonehenge area. This is very strange, since they are of different ages. Was this a routine pattern of movement, in which children were sent to a different region later in childhood? Or had these related men been born and grown up around the same time and then moved to the Stonehenge region together, before dying at different ages, and then those who had died earlier were reburied with the last one when he finally passed away?

These three burials show how people travelled to the Stonehenge area from great distances. Clearly, the ritual landscape and mortuary monuments of this region held a powerful attraction. The story of the Amesbury Archer, his Companion and the Boscombe Bowmen provides a small snapshot of the people who lived during the late third millennium BC in southern England. Archaeology is a collection of such snapshots, a few crisply focused, most very blurry. Let us now back up a few thousand years and zoom out to include more space and time to examine the changes in Stone Age society that culminated in the people who made the Bell Beakers.[3]

After the ice

By about 10,000 years ago, the ice sheets that had covered much of northern Europe had retreated back to northern Scandinavia. Forests sprang up over regions that until recently had been covered by ice and tundra. The glaciers left the landscape dotted with lakes, and rivers carved new courses on their way to the sea. The new forests were full of game and edible plants, while rivers, lakes and seas teemed with fish and other aquatic animals as well as being magnets for waterfowl. Vast colonies of seals sprang up along the coasts. Stone Age people who lived by hunting, gathering, fishing and collecting quickly recognized the possibilities that these rich resources presented.

The coastlines of northern Europe were still changing; hunters could still walk from Denmark to England. Ireland, however, became separated very soon after the glacial retreat, which is why no snakes lived there. The Baltic Sea started as a freshwater lake fed by retreating glaciers, but rising global sea levels eventually overcame the land bridge between Denmark and Sweden. The North Sea basin was eventually flooded as well. By about 7,500 years ago, the European coastline looked much more modern, although parts of Scandinavia freed from the crushing burden of ice continue to move upward even today, resulting in further changes to the coastline.

The post-glacial hunter-gatherers of temperate Europe adapted their technology to new environmental conditions. These included new types of stone tools that made more efficient use of flint resources when embedded in handles of wood and antler. Antler was also used for making harpoons. A very clever and effective fish spear was called a 'leister'. Leisters were composite tools, consisting of two curving and barbed pieces of antler and a bone or

Bottom of a Stone Age dugout canoe on the seabed at Ronæs Skov, Denmark.

wood point attached to a wooden handle. When thrust downward over the back of a fish spotted in the clear water, the antler pieces would grip the fish at the sides and the point would pin it in place just long enough for it to be pulled from the water. Combinations of materials, such as flint with wood, to make composite tools represented a major advance over Ice Age technology.

Mastery of wood was a hallmark of these Stone Age communities. Much of it was used to make equipment for fishing. Conical traps into which fish (especially eels) could swim but not escape were made with willow, dogwood or hazel branches. Wooden fences of stakes and branches were built across shallow bays. At high tide, fish could swim over them, but at low tide they would be stranded and could be collected. Such facilities permitted catching of fish on an immense scale. They required concepts of property and ownership, since people would not invest time in building and maintaining them if the fish could simply be taken by others.

In the watery world of northern Europe, Stone Age people regarded streams, rivers, lakes and calm seas as places for hunting and catching, as well as routes for movement so they could position themselves to get the most out of the environment. They developed new watercraft as well as the equipment needed to use them effectively. Dugout canoes made from tree trunks appear in the archaeological record around 8000 BC, usually in waterlogged sites like bogs, lakeshores and shallow bays. Along with canoes, wooden paddles have also been found. At the Danish site of Tybrind Vig, about a dozen paddles made mainly from ash wood were discovered.[4] Some were decorated by carving, stamping and painting, indicating that their owners not only considered them to be tools but also a medium for artistic expression.

The development of watercraft and their associated technology permitted hunters and collectors to travel much further from home, but at the same time they could maintain settlements without having to relocate often, perhaps even throughout the year. Here, they could use large fixed structures like fish traps rather than carry their equipment from place to place. The concept of a place to call home replaced the idea of a territory or home range. Some locations, like the 'kitchen midden' shell mounds along the shores of Denmark, were heavily used, presumably by a resident community.

Another indication of an attachment to particular places is provided by the development of cemeteries during the sixth and fifth millennia BC, such as the ones found at Skateholm in Sweden, Zvejnieki in Latvia and Oleneostrovskii Mogilnik in Russia. Great care was taken with burying the dead. Many bodies were sprinkled with red ochre (iron oxide), while deer antlers and flint tools were often placed in graves. At Skateholm, dogs were buried with the same care as people,[5] indicating their importance as companions and guardians.

The post-glacial hunters, fishers and gatherers of northern Europe are now recognized for their creativity in adapting to new environmental conditions and developing new social arrangements. Their way of life was quite successful. Deer, wild pigs, fish and hazelnuts provided a reliable supply of food. In fact, the abundance of resources from the forests and oceans may have contributed to a delay in the adoption of agriculture by Stone Age communities across much of northern and western Europe.

Farmers in the forests

Around the same time that ice was disappearing from northern Europe, prehistoric communities in the Near East began intensively harvesting certain plant species and controlling certain animal species. Around 11,000 years ago, the selection for desirable characteristics in wheat and barley and in sheep and goats began to manifest itself in the archaeological record in the Levant and the hills of Turkey and Syria.[6] Later, cattle, pigs, lentils and peas were also domesticated. These plants and animals formed what could be called the 'founder crops' and 'founder livestock' of the earliest Old World agriculture. From this core area, domestic plants and animals, as well as the embrace of the changes in human society that such a transformation entailed, spread outward to North Africa, southwest Asia and Europe.

The spread of farming to Europe began about 9,000 years ago, or just after 7000 BC, from Anatolia to Greece.[7] All the principal

Reconstruction of the burials of two young Stone Age women at Téviec, Brittany, France, showing shell necklaces and deer antlers.

plants and animals used by the earliest European farmers were first domesticated in the Near East. In some cases, farming communities migrated to settle new fertile soils, while elsewhere hunter-gatherers chose to settle down and adopt crops and livestock. From Greece, we can trace the spread of farming and farmers northward and westward through the appearance of the bones of domestic animals, charred grains and distinctive pottery. By 6000 BC we find agricultural communities in Italy and in the Danube valley. A millennium later, they had reached the Atlantic and the English Channel.

Within the area that we are calling the Barbarian World, the first farmers settled fertile soils in the river basins of central Europe like those of the Danube, the Rhine, the Elbe and the Vistula. They made distinctive incised pottery, and their settlements have traces of large timber houses, sometimes over 21 metres (70 ft) long.

These longhouses were the largest free-standing buildings in the world 7,000 years ago.[8] Their inhabitants grew wheat, barley and peas and kept mainly cattle, unlike the early farmers in Greece and the Balkans, where sheep and goats were the main livestock. Chemical analyses of ceramics have shown that cattle were used for milk as well as for meat. Not all was happy, however, and evidence of massacres at Talheim and Schöneck-Kilianstädten in Germany indicates that the early farmers had a violent side.[9]

The hunter-gatherers who lived along the coasts of northern Europe in 5000 BC, with their abundant resources, did not immediately find much attraction in agriculture. Hunting, fishing and collecting were more than adequate for their needs. For over 1,000 years, they continued their way of life. Around 4000 BC, however, something led them to adopt domestic plants and animals. The reasons for this transition in Scandinavia and the British Isles are unclear. Something disrupted the hunter-gatherer economy,

Original wooden piles in Lac de Chalain, rive occidentale (FR-39-02) with the reconstruction of a Stone Age dwelling in the background.

perhaps climate change or a new technology like dairying, that ultimately caused the adoption of farming in northwestern Europe. By 3000 BC farming could be found as far north as the Shetland Islands and to the limit of the growing season for early wheat. A similar transition took place in the Alpine regions of central Europe, where agricultural communities were established on the shores of lake basins in Switzerland and adjacent parts of Germany, France, Austria and Italy starting just before 4000 BC. The story of the 'Swiss Lake Dwellings', which follows below, is a case study in the history of archaeology and in modern analytical approaches.

Lake views at the foot of the Alps

During the cold and dry winter of 1853–4, lake levels near Zürich dropped. The receding water revealed a layer of black sediment, out of which rows of wooden posts protruded. The sediment layer contained animal bones, antlers, pottery and objects made from wood, bone, antler and flint. Since the local schoolteacher collected antiquities, the residents brought it to his attention, and he in turn notified Ferdinand Keller (1800–1881) of the Antiquarian Society in Zürich.[10]

Keller realized that the posts were parts of structures and the artefacts were the traces of prehistoric settlement. Unlike dryland sites, the waterlogged finds from the Zürich lakes were exceptionally well preserved and included hides and textiles, seeds and fruits. The fact that they had been submerged was also unusual. There was no question that these were prehistoric sites, but the question of 'how old?' was not easily answered. Keller first attributed them to 'Celts', and thus began public fascination with the 'Swiss Lake Dwellings'.

Seeing the posts sticking out of the lake mud, Keller proposed that the houses were built offshore on platforms, connected to the shore with gangplanks, and their residents simply pitched rubbish into the water. He called them 'pile dwellings', or *Pfahlbauten* in German. It is not certain where he got this idea, but around the same time, travellers were reported seeing pile dwellings on lakes in Malaya and the East Indies. He may also have heard about Irish and Scottish sites called 'crannogs' built on artificial islands in lakes.

The romantic vision of prehistoric people living on platforms fired the imagination of the public, and archaeologists embraced it as well. Paintings and models depicted pile dwellings fancifully, with happy people living an idyllic life. Over time, it became clear that the inhabitants of these sites were farmers, since the sediments yielded bones of domestic animals and plants, along with many wild species, but most of them lacked metal finds. Wooden artefacts included picks, hoes, sickles, axe handles and arrows. Fishing nets, baskets, ropes and textiles were made from plant and animal fibres.

During the late nineteenth century and early twentieth century, more waterlogged settlements were discovered around the Alpine foothills. Excavation techniques in early years were crude, but more refined methods and better understanding of how lake levels changed over the centuries led to reappraisal of the idea of houses built on platforms over open water. Traces of hearths and floors were identified among the posts. By the middle of the twentieth century, the idea of wooden islands was discarded, and archaeologists accepted the idea that the settlements had been built on the lakeshores. Since the ground was wet and soft, the posts that formed the structural elements were driven deep to keep the buildings from sinking. As lake levels rose, the bottoms of the posts and the domestic rubbish deposits were covered by water and preserved.

New methods of excavation and analysis, as well as the frequent discovery of new sites, make the lake dwellings an important area of current research. Arbon-Bleiche 3 lies submerged in a shallow bay on the south shore of Lake Constance. We know that this shoreline settlement was occupied between 3384 and 3370 BC based on the tree rings of the timbers.[11] The inhabitants of 27 houses grew wheat, barley, peas, flax and opium poppy and collected elderberries and hazelnuts. They raised pigs, sheep and cattle, hunted deer and wild pigs and caught many kinds of fish. A typical house at Arbon-Bleiche was about 4 by 8 metres (13 × 26 ft), with walls made from branches plastered with clay and sealed with moss. A fire swept the settlement around 3370 BC, and due to rising lake levels it was not rebuilt. Arbon-Bleiche 3 is an excellent example in which the combination of remarkable preservation, modern analytical methods and the ability to date finds precisely using tree rings has advanced our knowledge of early European farmers.

Wheeled vehicles

The Stone Age caveman chipping a wheel from a block of stone is a figment of the cartoonist's imagination. In reality, wheels and wheeled vehicles were invented around 4000–3500 BC, and there is considerable evidence for their early use in central and northern Europe. Before getting to the wheel, it was necessary to have something to pull the wagon, and the use of oxen for traction began during the late fifth millennium BC. The recognition that large domestic animals could be used for their power was as significant a development as agriculture itself.

Evidence for early wheels comes in three forms: actual wooden wheels preserved in waterlogged deposits; models or depictions of wheels and wagons; and rutted tracks made by repeated passes of wheeled vehicles.[12] The waterlogged lake-dwelling sites of Alpine Europe have yielded almost two dozen preserved wheels dating to the fourth and third millennia BC. Most were made from three boards (usually maple) connected by strips of wood (usually ash) fitted tightly into slots across the joints. Representations of wagons on pottery and models are found a bit further east. A vessel at Bronocice in Poland from about 3500 BC had a schematic image of a four-wheeled wagon, while several ceramic wagon models are known from Hungarian sites like Budakalász. A pair of oxen made from copper was found at Bytyń in Poland, unfortunately without a precise date but probably from the third millennium BC. Finally, ruts interpreted as having been caused by ancient wheeled vehicles have been found at Flintbek in northern Germany.

The invention of wheeled vehicles had important consequences for the lives of early farming communities. Draft animals – for drawing heavy loads – would have been major investments, and a family that owned them would be significantly wealthier than one that did not. Initially, wheeled vehicles probably simplified life close to home, enabling a family to transport crops from fields and firewood from the woods with less effort. Eventually, they came to be used over longer distances.

Copper metallurgy

Beginning in the sixth millennium BC in the Balkans but starting in earnest during the fourth millennium elsewhere in central Europe, Stone Age farmers began to mine and smelt copper in order to make artefacts and tools. In order to do this, they had to achieve very high temperatures. Pure copper melts at 1981°F (1083°C), and thus pottery technology had to advance sufficiently to attain such high heat. When copper ore is heated above this point, the metal separates from impurities. It can then be hammered into strips and sheets, which were used by Stone Age people to form artefacts such as beads, bracelets and pendants, or it can be cast in moulds to make larger objects like axes.

Copper ores like malachite and azurite occur in very specific locations.[13] In northern Europe, the best-studied sources are found in the eastern Alps, in the Harz mountains of central Germany, in northern Wales and in southwestern Ireland. Mines were dug into the sides of mountains, where seams of ore were heated and then doused with cold water to crack the rock. From these sources, smelted copper was passed on to metalsmiths, who shaped it into ornaments and tools.

Copper has one major problem. Unless alloyed with tin or arsenic to make bronze, it is very soft. A copper awl or punch simply bends, and a copper dagger or axe would have a limited life if it was actually used for chopping or cutting. For that reason, copper, which would have been very shiny and attractive when new, was used mainly for ornaments to demonstrate that the wearer had access to an exotic material. Tools made from copper, while functional up to a point, were probably more valuable as status markers than for felling trees. The good thing, however, is that

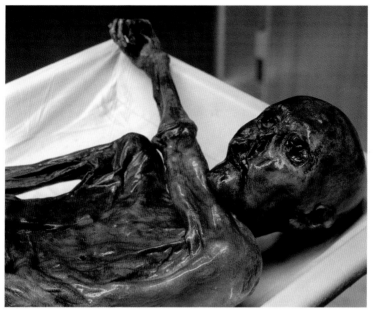

The famous ice mummy known as Ötzi, or The Iceman.

copper can be melted down and reused, thus making it a durable material for Stone Age farmers who wished to acquire tangible objects of value.

The Iceman's story

In September 1991, two German hikers walking in the Alps on the border between Austria and Italy made a grisly discovery that transformed our understanding of life in prehistoric Europe during the fourth millennium BC. Protruding from slush in an icy gully were the head and torso of a male corpse. Now, 25 years after his discovery, the Iceman, as he is known, continues to provide scientists with new evidence about his life and times.[14]

Although the corpse was roughly handled by well-meaning responders, not until after it was transported to Innsbruck in Austria and the site was examined forensically did it begin to dawn that the Iceman might be a prehistoric person. Artefacts found with the corpse included objects of wood, leather, flint and grass, along with a metal axe. Based on the shape of the axe, it was initially believed that the corpse was about 4,000 years old. Even such a dating would have made it exceptionally old, so efforts were made to preserve it, and samples were sent for carbon-14 dating.

The radiocarbon dates caused a sensation. All pointed towards a date of about 3300 BC. Moreover, metallurgical testing of the axe showed that it was pure copper, consistent with the age indicated by the carbon-14 dating. Thus, the Iceman turned out to be someone who lived during the Stone Age, during the fourth millennium BC, when copper was just coming into use in southern Europe. Other objects found in the gully turned out to be things that the Iceman was carrying or wearing. Most had been never been encountered previously by archaeologists. The Iceman himself posed many questions: Where did he come from? Where was he going? Why was he so high in the Alps? How did he die?

The establishment of the Iceman's age resulted in extensive media coverage, and the 5,300-year-old corpse became a celebrity. Since he was found near the Ötztaler glacier, he was nicknamed 'Ötzi' in the German-language press, although archaeologists still refer to him as the Iceman. After some time it was determined that he had actually been found on the Italian side of the poorly marked border, so after study in Innsbruck, the Iceman and his belongings were returned to Italy and placed in a museum in Bolzano.[15]

Details about the Iceman himself soon emerged. He had been short, about 160 centimetres (5 ft 3 in.) tall, and weighed about 50 kilograms (110 lb), but was relatively old for his time, at over forty. On his back, knees, ankles and left wrist were tattoos, made by rubbing charcoal into small cuts: when the cuts healed, charcoal dust remained in the skin. The tattoos are in groups of short lines, and on one knee they formed a cross. Although his teeth were worn, he had no cavities. Yet, Ötzi had lived a hard life. Various bones had been broken and healed, and he suffered from arthritis. His toes had been frostbitten repeatedly. His lungs had been blackened by a lifetime of inhaling smoke, and his arteries were clogged. Recently, the bacterium *Helicobacter pylori* has been identified in the Iceman's stomach, which could have caused inflammation.[16]

The contents of the Iceman's digestive system yielded a mixture of meat and wheat, along with other species of plants.[17] The wheat provided clear indication that he came from an agricultural community, but the meat was from red deer and ibex rather than domestic species. His last meal consisted of Alpine ibex meat, consumed an hour or less before he died. Pollen in Ötzi's digestive tract included hazel, birch, pine and hop hornbeam. Hop hornbeam grows south of the Alps, so it is clear that the Iceman had been in a valley in northern Italy before he died. In addition, the presence of hop hornbeam pollen shows the season in which Ötzi died, for this tree flowers in the spring.

Prior to the discovery of the Iceman, archaeologists had no idea of what Stone Age people wore. Ötzi was dressed for the cold. His cap and the soles of his shoes were made from bear fur. A coat, leggings and a loincloth were made from goatskin, while deer hide was used for the upper parts of his shoes. His belt and a pouch were made of calfskin. The most unusual discovery was that the Iceman was wearing a sleeveless cloak made from tufts of Alpine grass bound together with grass twine. This was worn on top of the other garments and probably would have been warm and water-repellent.

Each article of clothing had some unusual feature. The coat is made of small pieces of goatskin sewn together, while a deerskin strap had been attached to the leggings to keep them from riding up. The calfskin belt that held up the loincloth was long, about 2 metres (6½ ft), so it must have gone around Ötzi at least twice. His bearskin cap had two leather straps that tied under the chin. The shoes were complicated, consisting of an oval leather sole, a net of twisted grass around the foot, grass insulation held in place by the net and a piece of deerskin across the top. They were probably difficult to put on but look warm.

The Iceman was carrying a lot of equipment. His copper axe had been set in a handle made from a yew branch about 60 centimetres (2 ft) long with a shorter branch extending from one end. The short branch had been split to hold the axe blade, which was anchored in place with birch pitch, then wrapped tightly with leather straps. Ötzi was also carrying a yew bow, which was curiously unfinished. A quiver made from chamois skin held fourteen arrows made from a tough wood known as viburnum. Only two

The Iceman's copper axe-head.

had points attached. It appears that the Iceman was carrying a backpack with a hazel frame covered with leather, although it was in such fragmentary condition that reconstruction is difficult.

Ötzi's death has been the subject of morbid fascination. The initial hypothesis was that he had simply been caught in a snowstorm and died of exposure. Then, a decade after he was found, a CT scan of his left shoulder discovered a small flint arrowhead that had been hidden from X-rays by his shoulder blade.[18] A tiny unhealed entrance wound indicated where it struck him. The arrow lacerated his subclavian artery, resulting in massive bleeding and eventually cardiac arrest.

Who shot Ötzi? During his final two days, according to study of the pollen in his intestine, he was first in an area of pine and spruce forest. Then he descended to a valley in which hop horn-beam grew. Several hours before he died, he trekked upwards again, through the pine and spruce woods and then beyond the tree line, where he ate his last meal before being shot. Was he being pursued? If so, why did he stop to eat? Did someone ambush him there? If so, why did they not take his valuable copper axe? Was he killed in retribution for a crime or in a feud?

All these questions are motivated by the fact that we know so much more about the Iceman than about any other person of his time, and these details have permitted a narrative to be spun around him. His death reflects the violence endemic in Stone Age society, but he lived in a technologically advanced world, as indicated by his copper axe and yew bow. Note the tremendous diversity in the species of wood used for his equipment and of animals used for his clothing. Ötzi's tattoos carried a message for other people in his community. He was mobile and accustomed to moving around in the valleys, foothills and peaks of the Alps. Thanks to Ötzi, we can now glimpse the people behind the pot-sherds, flint tools and early metal artefacts.

Testimony of the stones

While Ötzi was living and dying in the Alps, and while people in southern Germany and Switzerland built their lakeside dwellings, the inhabitants of northern and western Europe erected burial monuments from large stones. These stones were set vertically to form corridors and chambers, which were then roofed with more flat stones before the whole structure was covered with a mound of earth and rocks. These constructions are known as passage graves and dolmens, both of which are types of 'chambered tombs' that, in turn, along with standing stones, constitute the scope of megalithic monuments, or megaliths (from the Greek for 'large stone'). They are the most visible traces of the Barbarian World from the fourth and third millennia BC in northern and western Europe.[19]

Several regions of northwestern Europe are especially luminous when it comes to megalithic monuments, although many have been destroyed over the last five millennia. In Ireland, passage graves are clustered into several groups, called megalithic cemeteries, while others lie on isolated mountaintops. Brittany is a megalithic paradise, with complicated passage graves and standing stones known as menhirs. The Orkney Islands far to the north are dotted with passage graves and stone circles. Denmark and Sweden also have concentrations of passage graves and dolmens, while across the Netherlands and northern Germany, large graves known as *Hunebedden* are found in forests and sandy areas. Dolmens occur down the Atlantic coast as far as Spain and Portugal.

The Irish cemeteries

Chambered tombs are found throughout Ireland, but four clusters of passage graves stand out from the others. At Carrowmore near Sligo, a megalithic cemetery lies in the shadow of a huge passage grave on top of Knocknarea Mountain. The view from Knocknarea in the other direction looks out over the wild Atlantic. About 30 kilometres (19 mi.) southeast at Carrowkeel, several peaks are covered with small tombs. To the east, 75 kilometres (47 mi.) from Carrowkeel, more than thirty passage graves dot several hilltops at Loughcrew. Finally, another 50 kilometres (30 mi.) east lie the celebrated passage graves of the Boyne Valley, including Newgrange, only a few kilometres inland from the east coast of Ireland. These four large megalithic cemeteries form a belt across Ireland from west to east, all dating from the second half of the fourth millennium BC.[20]

The Boyne Valley group is the most famous Irish passage grave cemetery.[21] At a bend in the river Boyne, called *Brú na Bóinne* in Irish, the tombs of Knowth, Dowth and Newgrange form focal points of a vast mortuary and ceremonial complex that flourished around 3200 BC. Of the three, Newgrange is the best known, for both its size and architecture, as well as for the fact that on the winter solstice the rising sun shines directly down its passage into the central chamber. Newgrange is a round mound about 85 metres (280 ft) in diameter and 11 metres (36 ft) high, outlined by 97 large blocks of stone, some decorated with engraved spirals. Based on interpretation of rocks scattered around the tomb entrance, the southern facade of Newgrange was reconstructed in the 1980s as a wall of bright white quartz and grey granite boulders. As a result, it now looks unlike any other passage grave, and the highly improbable reconstruction has been widely criticized. Nonetheless, the modern appearance of Newgrange, whether it reflects prehistoric reality or the imagination of an archaeologist, has become fixed in the public perception of how it should look.[22]

Entering the tomb and half-crawling, half-slouching down the passage, past upright stones called orthostats averaging about 1.5 metres (5 ft) high, the visitor reaches the chamber, which is about 5.2 × 6.6 metres (17 × 22 ft).Here it is possible to stand. Looking up, one can see the corbelled roof, in which courses of flat stones were laid progressively closer to the centre until the ceiling was closed about 6 metres (20 ft) above the floor. Cells opening off the main chamber give it a cross-shaped plan.

We know little about what the burial chamber contained. Newgrange has been entered by visitors since at least 1699, and only a few cremated bones remained until modern times between the stones. Based on what we know from undisturbed Irish passage tombs, such as the Mound of the Hostages at Tara,[23] the chamber and side cells probably contained cremated burials, as such was the burial rite at this time in Stone Age Ireland, along with an assortment of pottery and enigmatic artefacts known as 'mushroom-headed pins' made from animal bone.

The most important aspects of Newgrange are its location and orientation. Its hilltop site made it visible from a great distance, whether or not it had a shiny facade. We can assume that it was a centre of communal ritual and mortuary activity. The orientation of the entrance so that the sun shines down the passage on the winter solstice is clearly deliberate. From 19 to 23 December, starting at dawn and lasting about seventeen minutes, a beam of sunlight shines through an opening above the entrance and moves up the floor of the passage into the chamber. Stone Age builders must

The passage grave at Newgrange with its reconstructed, and improbable,
quartz facade.

Entrance to the passage grave at Newgrange showing the carved entrance stone and the opening above, into which the sun shines at dawn on the winter solstice.

have determined this alignment in a previous year, marked it and then consciously incorporated it into the design of the tomb.

The other exceptional feature of Irish passage graves is the appearance of an ornate style of carving and pecking on rocks to produce curvilinear, zigzag and especially spiral motifs. This is the celebrated 'megalithic art style' seen in modern evocations of the 'Celtic' spirit on everything from Irish sugar packets to the stage scenery of *Riverdance*. The spiral motif is the most common. Although the kerbstones that surround the mound at Knowth have the greatest single concentration of megalithic art in Ireland, the ornate entrance stone at Newgrange is perhaps the most memorable example of this abstract style of ornament.

Apotheosis of the Stone Age

Perhaps the most iconic site of prehistoric Europe lies on Salisbury Plain in southern England. Stonehenge is celebrated in art, film,[24] literature and the popular imagination. Images of the massive stones taken from the perspective of a visitor make it appear huge and monumental, which to a certain degree it is. The fact that these stones were erected using Stone Age technology baffles those who think of pre-literate peoples as primitive. From a distance, Stonehenge is still distinctive, but to a visitor coming over a rise on the A303 road, the first impression is really how tiny it is when sitting within its broader landscape.

The surrounding landscape is a crucial part of the Stonehenge story. Its great stones can only be understood as part of an immense ceremonial landscape stretching outward in every direction towards the edge of the shallow bowl in which Stonehenge sits and down to the nearby river Avon. This appreciation of the Stonehenge environs comes from intensive archaeological investigation that ramped up in the late 1990s and continues today. New discoveries are announced almost annually, so anything written more than a year or two ago is by definition incomplete.[25]

Stonehenge, so named from an Anglo-Saxon root that means 'hanging', perhaps due to its resemblance to a gallows,[26] was always visible throughout later prehistory and medieval times, but there is no record of it being of great significance as a ceremonial site after about 1500 BC. It was 'rediscovered' by antiquarians of the seventeenth and eighteenth century like John Aubrey and William Stukeley, who worked it into their narratives about the early Britons. The evocative image of the standing and tumbled stones against the horizon was a favourite subject of artists like John Constable in the nineteenth century. Today, Stonehenge appears in the news every summer solstice when devotees of New Age spirituality converge at sunrise.

The megaliths seen at Stonehenge today were erected in the second half of the third millennium BC, but it is necessary to understand that the monument had an earlier incarnation just after 3000 BC. At this time, a circular ditch with an interior bank about 100 metres (328 ft) in diameter was constructed.[27] Around the interior perimeter, 56 holes were dug into the chalk. These are known as the Aubrey Holes, after the antiquarian John Aubrey, who found them in the seventeenth century. For centuries, they were an enigma, but recent investigation has shown that they were footings for small, upright stones. Known as 'bluestones', these came from the Presceli mountains in Wales 160–240 kilometres (100–150 mi.) away. Thus, the first edition of Stonehenge looked little like the monument on the same location today, although it had counterparts in stone circles elsewhere in the British Isles.

Recent research has shown the extent to which this first version of Stonehenge functioned as a cemetery.[28] Cremated remains of over sixty individuals have been excavated from its interior. We do not know what merited their burial at a large stone circle and ditched enclosure, although the effort required to bring the bluestones from Wales clearly marked this spot as having a connection with a distant place. The cremations were deposited over the first half of the third millennium BC, although it is not yet clear whether this was episodic or continuous mortuary activity.

About 500 years after the construction of the initial monument at Stonehenge, major expansion and remodelling took place, between 2620 and 2480 BC. First to go up was a horseshoe-shaped pattern of five immense 'trilithons' consisting of two upright blocks and a lintel. Erecting these presented a major technical challenge at every stage. First, the blocks of sandstone known as 'sarsen' had to be quarried from an outcrop, probably to the north near Avebury. Second, they were chipped and pecked into their rectangular cuboid shape with a tenon sticking out of one end. Third, they had to be transported to Stonehenge, where pits had been excavated for them. They would have been too heavy for rollers directly on soft ground, so it is likely that a wooden platform to

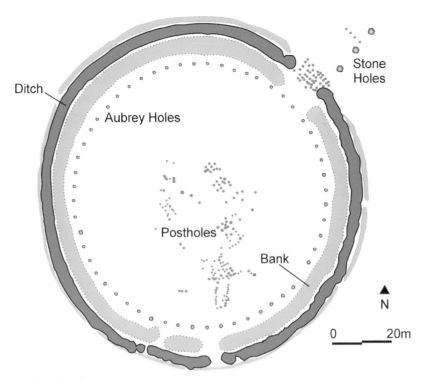

Plan of Stonehenge in stage 1 during the early third millennium BC.

distribute the load must have been built, which in turn was on rollers that ran on timber rails. Power from oxen was necessary. Fourth, they needed to be set upright into the pits, a dangerous process which also had to ensure that they were vertical. Finally, the lintels, with mortises cut into their undersides, had to be raised above the height of the uprights, moved over the tenons and lowered into place, with the hope that the whole edifice was balanced so it did not topple over.

After the trilithons were in place, the outer circle of sarsen uprights and continuous lintels went up. Finally, bluestones from the Aubrey Holes were relocated to the centre of the monument to form further circular arrangements within the two sarsen settings. During this construction phase, other standing stones in the Stonehenge complex such as the Station Stone and the Heel Stone were probably also erected. Stonehenge continued in use as a cremation cemetery during this time. When the Amesbury

Archer and the Boscombe Bowmen arrived about a century later, they saw Stonehenge functioning within its ceremonial landscape.

Further modifications of Stonehenge continued for the rest of the third millennium BC and even into the start of the second millennium. These relatively smaller remodelling episodes took place against a backdrop of changes in the surrounding monumental landscape, which in turn reflect the social milieu within which Stonehenge functioned. This leads to the other half of the Stonehenge story, its larger ceremonial landscape, largely hidden due to the fact that other monuments were built in timber or with stones that were subsequently removed.

Mortuary activity had already taken place around Stonehenge even before the first bank and ditch there. Long mounds at Netheravon Bake and Amesbury 42 were built around 3600 BC, around the same time as the famous West Kennet long barrow 37 kilometres (23 mi.) to the north. In 2014, geophysical surveys discovered an even earlier earthen long barrow, probably also from the fourth millennium BC, with a complex interior timber structure and a timber forecourt in front of its entrance.[29]

Considerable structuring of the landscape had also taken place before the first monument was built at Stonehenge itself. Two linear bank and ditch features to the north of Stonehenge called the Greater Cursus and the Lesser Cursus are so named because they seemed to resemble Roman racing tracks. The Greater Cursus is about 3 kilometres (1.9 mi.) long and 100 metres (330 ft) wide, running west–east, while the Lesser Cursus is a smaller feature to its northwest. Geophysical surveys have recently found two immense pits within the Greater Cursus near its ends, each about 5 metres (16 ft) wide. About 2 kilometres (1.25 mi.) east of Stonehenge, a small circle of bluestones about 10 metres (33 ft) across was erected.

Most of the construction of the Stonehenge ceremonial landscape took place when the trilithons and sarsens were erected. Two timber circles were set up at Durrington Walls, 3.2 kilometres (2 mi.) northeast of Stonehenge. The southern one is more complex, starting from a simple timber circle to six concentric rings with additional interior patterning that might reflect the stones at

Stonehenge. Near Durrington Walls is Woodhenge, again with six concentric post settings in an oval pattern. Additional mini-henges are found nearby, and geophysical surveys keep finding more. In many respects, Stonehenge can be considered the exception in stone of a larger class of monuments mostly made from wood.

Recent research at Durrington Walls has also brought to light traces of human habitation in the form of houses and rubbish deposits, which appear to date from around 2535–2475 BC. The Durrington Walls houses were small and square, about 5.25 metres (17 ft) on each side. No burials have yet come to light. Of special interest is the huge collection of animal bones, around 80,000, from the rubbish deposits.[30] They consisted largely of pig and cattle bones, in an unusual ratio of 9:1 pigs to cattle. Most of the pigs were killed either at nine months or at fifteen months, so in the early summer or midwinter assuming they were born in the spring. Some of the cattle were brought from other parts of Britain, based on strontium isotope ratios. The habitation traces at Durrington Walls are interpreted as short-term occupations associated with feasting, suggesting that this was not a permanent community but rather temporary visitors.

Many archaeologiests now believe that during the middle of the third millennium BC, Stonehenge on the chalk plateau in the west and Durrington Walls in the valley of the Avon on the east were the anchors of a complex ceremonial landscape that was continually being revised. It was dotted with timber henges and other bank and ditch structures. Sometime between 2480 and 2280 BC, the small bluestone henge at Durrington Walls was taken down, a ditched enclosure was built on the site, and an approach path to Stonehenge called The Avenue was constructed.

Two questions remain: how was this ceremonial landscape used, and what was the role of the astronomical alignments that have been perceived in it? Vince Gaffney has proposed that the multiple timber henges that surround Stonehenge functioned as a sort of pilgrimage circuit as worshippers made their way from shrine to shrine.[31] In my view, a modern analogy might be the Roman Catholic shrine at Kalwaria Zebrzydowska in southern Poland, at which small chapels around a larger church mark the

Stations of the Cross, the route taken by Christ on his way to crucifixion. After getting off the train, pilgrims make their way in prayer from chapel to chapel, sometimes ascending stairs on their knees. Whether or not the Stonehenge timber sanctuaries functioned in a similar way, it is clear that they were elements of a larger ritual landscape which offered visitors a rich assortment of opportunities.

In 1965, the astronomer Gerald Hawkins (1928–2003) claimed that Stonehenge had functioned as an observatory to predict

Classic view of Stonehenge in its final phase as seen today: trilithons and sarsens erected in the second half of the third millennium BC.

movements of the sun and moon.[32] His argument was met with scepticism by archaeologists but seized the public imagination. Over the intervening fifty years, links to the annual passage of the sun have been documented from Stonehenge and other Stone Age monuments, the most notable being Newgrange as described above.[33] At Stonehenge, the rising of the sun on the summer solstice over the Heel Stone and down the main axis of symmetry is complemented by the winter solstice sunset in the opposite direction. The two newly discovered huge pits on the Cursus align with the heelstone on the summer solstice as well. Rather than functioning as an observatory or calendar itself, however, it seems more likely that Stonehenge illustrates the extent to which celestial observation was embedded in the practices of Stone Age people. They were keen observers of the skies, and celestial events were taken as cause for ceremonies and feasting.

The Barbarian World at 2000 BC

By 2000 BC, sedentary agricultural communities had been established throughout Europe north of the Alps. They took different forms in different places: large, small, concentrated, dispersed, on lakeshores, on high ground, long-term and temporary. The domestic plants and animals on which they relied were largely the same: wheat and barley as the principal grains, peas and lentils as legumes and cattle, goats, sheep and pigs as the major livestock species. Cattle were used not just for their meat but also for milk and power, while sheep provided wool and milk. Pottery replaced baskets to permit storage of grains and liquids.

Although Stone Age people had become largely sedentary, this did not mean that they were completely immobile. On the contrary, they travelled quite a bit. Watercraft facilitated travel across rivers, along lowland streams and across sheltered straits. Adventurous seafarers could cross open seas. Across land, trails and pathways followed well-worn routes to connect concentrations of population. Raw materials and finished products were widely traded, and people were able to share ideas and learn from each other.

Where large stones were available, people built megalithic mortuary and ceremonial monuments, after first building long earthen mounds without stone architecture. The most common form was the passage grave, concentrated along the Atlantic Facade but also found in southern Scandinavia. Passage graves took many different forms, but the central idea of a stone corridor into a burial chamber was largely similar in all areas. Standing stones were also a widespread form of monument across this entire area, in alignments or circles. Around Stonehenge, many timber circles were also erected, forming a complex ceremonial landscape.

The use of copper moved progressively from southeastern Europe in the fifth millennium BC to reach northern and western Europe by the end of the third millennium BC. Copper is soft, best suited to making ornaments, although daggers and axes were also made from it. The copper axe carried by Ötzi the Iceman and the copper knives of the Amesbury Archer represent the most that can be done with pure copper in terms of practical implements. Nonetheless, familiarity with mining and smelting copper, and eventually casting, was fundamental to the mastery of metals that followed.

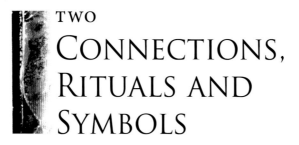

TWO
CONNECTIONS, RITUALS AND SYMBOLS

etween 2500 and 800 BC, prehistoric societies north of the Alps became more technologically sophisticated, leading to social and economic systems more complex than those seen during the Stone Age. This begins the second of Thomsen and Worsaae's three ages: the Bronze Age. Bronze enabled the manufacture of tools, weapons and ornaments in forms hitherto unimaginable, triggering a cascade of changes in transportation, social status and wealth reinforced by other novel materials and practices.

Today, most people do not know much about bronze, a material used largely for sculptures, church bells and specialized applications to avoid corrosion or sparks. Four thousand years ago, however, it was the industrial metal of choice, the result of experimentation and accumulated knowledge transmitted among metalsmiths throughout Europe. To make bronze requires knowledge of minerals, control of temperature, expertise in casting and the ability to recycle broken and worn-out products. Since bronze does not exist in nature, it represents the earliest example of what today we call materials science.

Bronze: the first engineered metal

Bronze is an alloy of copper and tin (sometimes arsenic or lead). Addition of tin to copper makes it much stronger and easier to cast. Moreover, the amount of tin can be varied to make the metal more or less hard depending on the desired use. For example, 10 per cent tin makes very hard bronze, good for weapons, while a milder 6 per cent bronze could be hammered into sheets to make body armour. As a result, the range of objects made from metal expanded dramatically. Their forms and decoration, reflecting the stylistic tastes of their makers, also multiplied.

The development of bronze 4,000 or more years ago can be compared to the invention of the microchip in the 1950s. Suddenly it was possible to make things that people had not even known they wanted and with a style that reflected their own identity and fashion sense. Different regions could make distinctive forms of weapons and ornaments, and to the joy of archaeologists 4,000 years in the future, these forms changed in response to shifts in taste and technological advances. Bronze could also be combined with traditional materials like wood or ornamental materials like gold and silver to make composite products.

Making bronze requires copper, and Europe north of the Alps has copper in abundance. It is rarely visible on the surface, so the mining of copper, a relatively limited practice during the Stone Age, started to take place on an industrial scale to meet the demand. Certain regions across temperate Europe became centres for copper mining.[1] In the Austrian Alps, the Mitterberg region south of Salzburg emerged as a major centre which produced several tons of copper per year for a number of centuries.[2] In this region, small settlements like the one at the Klinglberg that specialized in copper mining were established in defensible positions. At Great Orme in northern Wales, shafts and galleries were dug into the ore-bearing rocks. Other important mines were found in southwestern Ireland, for example at Mount Gabriel on the Mizen peninsula.

There was a catch, however. Tin is not usually found in the same places as copper. In fact, tin sources can be some distance away from copper ores and are usually very localized. During the Bronze Age, we know that tin deposits were exploited in Cornwall, Brittany and Spain. We have to be impressed by the ability of Bronze Age prospectors to find tin sources, and once they were found, to establish the trade connections to being the copper and tin together in the hands of smiths in central and northern Europe.

The result is a fascinating archaeological distribution of bronze artefacts across Europe that reflects centres of power and wealth rather than the distribution of raw materials. For example, while the mountains surrounding the Carpathian Basin have abundant copper deposits, there is no tin nearby, yet tremendous numbers of bronze artefacts dating to the second millennium BC have been found in Hungary, Austria and surrounding countries. Even more astonishing is the fact that Denmark lacks local deposits of *both* copper and tin, but there are probably more Bronze Age metal finds per square kilometre than in any other country north of the Alps.

Among many remarkable properties of bronze was its suitability for casting in moulds, and prehistoric smiths developed this expertise throughout the second millennium BC. Early open moulds were carved out of soft stones, but these were replaced by two-piece moulds made from stone and clay. Metalsmiths learned to include channels in the moulds into which molten bronze could be poured and through which the air in the mould could escape, which prevented bubbles in the finished product. Clay and wax cores made it possible to produce hollow objects or sockets into which a handle could be inserted. Moulds also permitted mass production: stone moulds could be reused dozens of times, and clay moulds could be formed around a prototype to make identical copies.

The variety and abundance of objects made by Bronze Age metalsmiths is astonishing. Weapons were in high demand, including daggers, swords, spear-points and many kinds of axe-heads. Axe shapes developed considerably over time. At the beginning of the Bronze Age, smiths continued to make flat axes like those used during previous centuries, only this time using the harder bronze. This was the cause of the initial assignment of Ötzi the Iceman to the Bronze Age, since his flat axe was first presumed to be from bronze rather than pure copper. Axes progressed to a form known as a palstave, which had a ridge halfway between the sharp edge and the blunt end that improved the attachment of a curved handle. Over time, the palstave was replaced by forms in which the handle was inserted into a socket moulded into the end of the axe-head. Thus the handle would not be split by striking a tree or a skull. Another nasty weapon was the halberd, which was like a dagger attached perpendicularly to a long handle.

Two remarkable Bronze Age objects are the so-called Sun Chariot from Trundholm in Denmark and the Nebra Disc found in southeastern Germany. The Sun Chariot has a moulded bronze horse on a four-wheeled platform pulling a bronze disc about 25 centimetres (10 in.) in diameter which has two additional wheels under it. The disc was plated with gold on one side and is covered with engraved designs. Dated to the second half of the second millennium BC, it was possibly made somewhere in central Europe. The Trundholm Sun Chariot currently appears on the Danish 1,000-krone banknotes issued in 2009.[3]

The Nebra Disc was found in a hoard of bronze objects by illegal metal-detectorists and was obtained by archaeologists after a sting operation. Thus its context is far from secure. Nonetheless, there is a strong consensus among archaeologists that the Nebra Disc is genuine and dates to the middle of the second millennium BC.[4] On a bronze disc about 32 centimetres (12 in.) in diameter, gold appliqués have been affixed. They clearly represent celestial bodies, including the sun, different stages of the moon and stars such as the Pleiades. The Nebra Disc is yet another indication of interest in the movement of celestial bodies by the inhabitants of the Barbarian World.

Everyday life in the Bronze Age

Despite the emergence of bronze metallurgy, everyday life for most people north of the Alps did not change much from previous millennia. Agricultural societies using the major domestic species of cereals, legumes and livestock flourished everywhere they could find fertile soil and ample pastures. Wheat and barley were the most widely cultivated plants, made into bread, porridge and beer. Legumes such as broad beans and peas were an important complement to cereals. Cattle, pigs, sheep and goats were kept in varying proportions from region to region, and the importance of milk and wool continued to grow. In many regions, herds of animals began to form the foundation for wealth rather than simply being

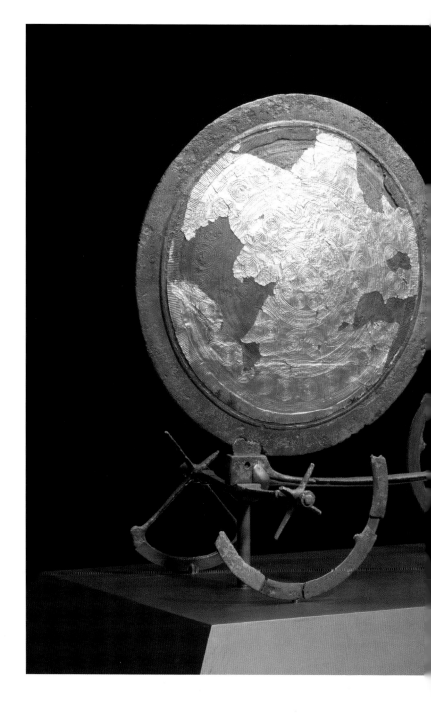

Bronze and gold 'sun chariot' from Trundholm, Denmark.

household possessions. Well-trained oxen or productive dairy cows could be exchanged for commodities or loaned to clients. It is not entirely clear when tamed horses, domesticated in central Asia during the fourth millennium BC, entered the Barbarian World for riding, although horse finds in bog offerings suggest that they were present by the end of the second millennium BC.

The archaeological record reveals a tremendous diversity of Bronze Age houses and settlements in Europe north of the Alps. A small farmstead with one or more houses, presumably the residence of one or more families, is the general form. They would have been surrounded by their fields and pastures. In general, these are dispersed across the landscape. More clustered settlements, what archaeologists would call 'nucleated', are rare.

In Denmark, the standard Bronze Age form was a long timber house with interior posts supporting the roof.[5] There is evidence that part of the interior space of these Danish houses was used for sheltering livestock. This practice is seen more clearly in the Netherlands, where longhouses were also the standard form and were clearly divided into stalls for animals and living space for people. The farmstead site at Elp was occupied repeatedly over several centuries, after being intermittently abandoned.

Bronze Age settlements in central Europe were quite varied. At Lovčičky in Moravia, substantial rectangular timber houses date to the late second millennium BC. Around the same time in Bavaria, a settlement at Hascherkeller consists of several compounds demarcated with ditches.[6] Wall daub and large pits interpreted as cellars point to the presence of houses, but unfortunately their outlines were eroded away. At a wetland settlement along the Federsee in southern Germany called Wasserburg Buchau, two phases of Late Bronze Age settlement were identified during excavations in the 1920s. The first consisted of 38 square houses, each side about 5 metres (16 ft) long, situated around an open plaza, while the second was composed of nine larger structures with a U-shaped plan.

In contrast to the longhouses of the Netherlands and southern Scandinavia, roundhouses were the standard Bronze Age house form in the British Isles, often grouped into farmsteads of two to ten houses built from stakes or small timbers. Sometimes they are

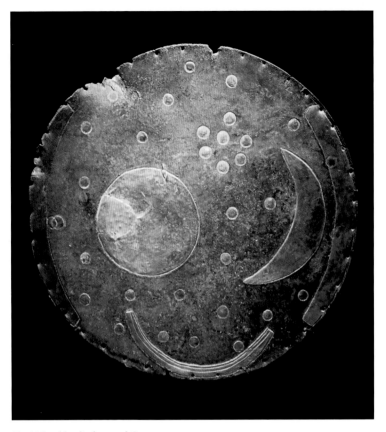

The Nebra 'sky disc', central Germany.

enclosed with a stone wall, as at Shaugh Moor in Dartmoor, where high phosphate levels in one of the structures indicate animals were kept in it. At Black Patch and Itford Hill in southeast England, small clusters of round huts about 8–12 metres (26–40 ft) in diameter were enclosed by fences to form compounds.

Bronze Age settlement is found in wetland areas in the British Isles, which is a bit baffling since these are not well suited for farming or livestock. At Clonfinlough, Co. Offaly, in Ireland, four wooden platforms 4–10 metres in diameter (13–33 ft) were built above a bog to support roundhouses dating to the Late Bronze Age. The platforms were connected by trackways and enclosed by an oval palisade. At Must Farm near Peterborough in eastern England, excavations in 2015 revealed that two roundhouses were built on platforms above or adjacent to an ancient stream channel, dating roughly to the same time as those at Clonfinlough.[7] The Must Farm houses had burned down, probably accidentally and unexpectedly, leaving evidence of hasty abandonment in the form of wooden bowls still containing food.

Bronze Age seafaring

The significance of watercraft during the Stone Age of northern Europe has already been mentioned, and mobility on water developed further during the Bronze Age.[8] On inland waters, dugout canoes continued in use, but the major advances came in seafaring. The transport of goods and people across straits and along coasts became commonplace. Narrow bodies of water like the English Channel and among the Baltic islands posed no obstacle. The Irish Sea has challenging conditions, but it seems that people could cross it regularly. Open seas, like the North Sea and the Atlantic between Ireland and Brittany, would have required navigation skills which were cultivated during the second millennium BC. Such transportation was necessary to link the copper and tin sources of the British Isles with the makers of bronze objects, and then to distribute finished bronze goods.

In northern Europe, we find shipwrecks and abandoned boats (many of which are close to shore or even on shore), cargoes on the seabed presumably dropped by sinking vessels that disintegrated, rock carvings and etchings and graves surrounded by large stones to form an outline of a ship. Several Bronze Age boats have been found in the British Isles dating between 2000 and 800 BC. They have a fairly uniform construction. Oak timbers were split into long planks which were then shaped with chisels and axes to join snugly. The planks were then stitched together using strips of yew, that same strong wood that was used for the Iceman's bow. Internal frames reinforced the shell. The use of sewn planks permitted the construction of very large boats. There is no evidence for masts or keels, so the inference is that these boats were paddled.

In 1992, road excavations near Dover in England exposed the remains of a boat abandoned around 1550 BC.[9] The recovered part was about 9 metres (30 ft) long and about 2.5 metres (8 ft) wide, but it is estimated that it originally may have been as much as 12 or even nearly 15 metres (40–50 ft) in length. Six huge sculpted planks were used for the body of the boat, two at the bottom and two on each side, with joints reinforced using additional strips of oak and caulked with moss. It is estimated that the Dover Boat held eighteen or more paddlers (and probably required more crew as bailers) and could ferry people, livestock and goods across the English Channel.

The Straits of Dover were a crucial point for cross-Channel commerce and travel, as is the case today. Paths and roads must have funnelled into a small area on both sides. In 1974, in Langdon

Dover Bronze Age boat, found during construction in September 1992 (as reconstructed).

Bay near Dover, more than 400 worn bronze tools and weapons from France were found on the seabed. Apparently this was a shipment headed for recycling in England, but the boat carrying it sank. The vessel itself has not been found, perhaps because it came apart, but the cargo fell to the bottom.

In Scandinavia, the principal evidence for seafaring comes in the form of over 10,000 recorded depictions of boats in rock carvings (discussed in greater detail below).[10] Usually these are found overlooking bays and inlets. Their form is fairly consistent. Two roughly parallel lines converge at the stem and stern when the lower one, representing the keel, turns upwards. The stern is usually indicated by a schematic rudder. People on the boat are portrayed either by tick marks or sometimes stick figures. Although the boat carvings are very schematic, the consensus is that they also represent plank boats. Their inclusion in compositions with cosmological significance indicates that seafaring was not only important economically but also ideologically.

Another indication of the importance of the boat in the cosmological order is the construction of stone settings around the graves of high-status individuals in parts of Scandinavia starting around 1300 BC, beginning a long tradition of 'ship settings' that lasted into the first millennium AD. In the ship-shaped graves, large standing stones have been arranged to imitate the outline of a ship in plan as well as in elevation. The tallest stones are placed at the stern and the keel, with the shortest at the middle of the boat. The ship burials usually contain the remains of one cremated individual, presumably of high social standing. Most are between about 2 metres (7 ft) and 16 metres (50 ft) long, but some very large ones are found at Gnisvärd on Gotland. Here, three large stone ships are arrayed in a line, as if sailing in formation. The largest is nearly 45 metres (150 ft) in length.

Paddled, plank-built boats played a crucial role in Bronze Age life in northwestern Europe, and they continued to do so during the millennia that followed as boatbuilding techniques developed. They were crucial for transporting raw materials and finished products, as well as enabling people to travel long distances across straits and seas. Their role in the rock-carving displays and as the outlines of elite graves shows just how important they were, as travel and ritual frequently came to intersect in the Barbarian World.

Death and burial in the Bronze Age

Much of our knowledge of the Bronze Age comes from burials. This fact skews our understanding of Bronze Age life, since artefacts deposited in graves were often lavish and costly. It is important to remember that mortuary rites are largely a performance for those who are still living. They may only indirectly reflect the status of the deceased individual. Only in cases of over-the-top displays of wealth in complex burial structures can we assume that the deceased had a level of status and power above most other members of a community. Nonetheless, many Bronze Age burials contain such quantities of finely worked metals, including gold, as well as objects of materials from distant sources or which required tremendous skill to fabricate, that they can be ascribed to elite individuals. A major question, however, is whether these elite burials marked the ascent of a long-term durable social hierarchy or whether they were short-term social practices.

At the beginning of the Bronze Age, the practice of burying individuals under mounds (also known as barrows or tumuli) that began during the third millennium BC in much of northern Europe continued. Typically, the corpse was placed in a small pit with other grave offerings, which was then covered with a mound. Over time, particular areas were defined as barrow cemeteries, such as the Haguenau forest in eastern France, where hundreds are found. In southern Scandinavia, Bronze Age burial mounds are silhouetted against the sky along higher parts of the landscape, whereas in Ireland the megalithic tradition continued in the construction of chambers known as wedge tombs, in which the slab forming the roof sloped downwards from one end to the other.

In the area surrounding Stonehenge and Durrington Walls, Early Bronze Age barrows on the surrounding ridgelines look down towards the monuments. About 400 barrows are known, almost all of which have a line of sight with either Stonehenge

Gnisvärd 'ship setting' Bronze Age burial monument on the island of Gotland.

or Durrington Walls. During the nineteenth century, it became fashionable to spend a Sunday afternoon digging into one of these barrows. Although this activity was often little more than grave-robbing, occasionally some investigators had a more serious interest in finding out about these graves.

In 1808, William Cunnington, wool merchant and amateur excavator, opened a barrow in a cluster of about forty mounds just south of Stonehenge at Normanton Down.[11] The mound, known as Bush Barrow, measured about 36.5 metres (120 ft) in diameter and was about 3.3 metres (10 ft) high when it was excavated. It contained a single, male skeleton lying on its left side in a crouched position. Two very large bronze daggers were in the grave, one with a wooden handle studded with gold-wire pins believed to have come from Brittany. Lying next to the body was a macehead made of rare flecked stone from Devon, and although its wooden shaft has decayed, its carved-bone decoration survives. Three gold objects were found, the most exceptional being a large diamond-shaped piece lying on the man's chest, decorated with delicate incised lines. Rivets and bronze fragments near the skeleton were the remains of a dagger dating 200 years earlier than the rest of the objects, perhaps the possession of an ancestor. We can say confidently that the man in Bush Barrow, as well as individuals under nearby mounds, belonged to an elite stratum of society.

Elite burials are also found in Continental Europe. The Leubingen barrow, excavated in the nineteenth century, covers a chamber about 4 by 2.2 metres (13 × 7 ft) made with a pitched roof of oak timbers. Under the wooden tent were two skeletons. One was a man about fifty years old, while draped across him was a younger woman. At his right shoulder and at his feet were gold ornaments, bronze tools and weapons and stone axes and pottery. The Leubingen barrow, and a similar one at Helmsdorf, are dated to the beginning of the second millennium BC. Elsewhere in this general part of central Europe, however, the standard burial rite involved placing the crouched corpses in rectangular pits, which are clustered into small cemeteries. The Leubingen and Helmsdorf elite burials have no real successors, so they do not seem to be the foundation of long-term social hierarchies.

Oak trees were used in a different way in Denmark during the second half of the second millennium BC. Massive oak trunks were split and hollowed out to create coffins whose lids formed an air-tight seal, assisted by water that did not drain out of the mound interior, creating anaerobic conditions. As a result, the contents of these coffins are extraordinarily well preserved, including cloth, leather and the deceased's hair.[12]

The most celebrated Danish Bronze Age coffin burial is that of a young woman about sixteen to eighteen years old from Egtved, found in a mound excavated in 1921. Her coffin was lined with cow-hide, and she was covered with a woollen blanket. Unfortunately, only her hair, brain, teeth, nails and a little skin remain of her body.

Egtved Girl is most famous for her clothing, which shows what fashionable young women wore in 1370 BC: a short woollen tunic on her torso and a knee-length, wrap-around skirt made from braided cord rather than woven cloth. Her hair was held in place with a woollen headband. Lying on her abdomen was a spiked bronze disc about 15 centimetres (6 in.) in diameter, decorated with concentric bands of spirals. Also in the coffin was a bundle containing the cremated remains of a child about six years old. Given Egtved Girl's age, it could not have been her child, so the relationship between her and the child is unknown. We know she was buried in the summer, since a yarrow flower was pressed between the two halves of the coffin when it was closed. A birch-bark container held the residue of a drink made from fermented honey, wheat and fruits, including cranberries.

The exceptional preservation of the girl in the Egtved coffin has recently enabled researchers using modern techniques to learn more details about her life.[13] As with the Amesbury Archer, strontium isotope ratios made it possible to determine where she spent her early years. But since her fingernails and hair were also preserved, it was possible to reconstruct her activities during the final months of her life. The strontium isotopes indicate that Egtved Girl was born several hundred kilometres away from where she was buried. Southeastern Germany, in the area of the Black Forest about 800 kilometres (500 mi.) to the south, has similar strontium isotope ratios, so the working hypothesis is that she came from that region. She seems to have moved back and forth between Jutland and the Black Forest regularly during her final months. Her hair, which documents her final two years, and her fingernails, which track her final six months, also show that she visited areas with strontium signatures similar to that of her home-land. The wool in which she was buried was also not produced locally.

Later in the second millennium BC, mortuary rites across much of the Barbarian World shifted from burial of the whole body to cremation. Across much of northern Europe, the cremated bones were placed in ceramic urns and buried in immense cemeteries that often contain hundreds, if not thousands, of burials. Rather

Borum Eshøj, Denmark; 19th-century drawing by Magnus Petersen of an oak coffin containing the body of an old man.

Woollen blouse and corded skirt worn by Egtved Girl.

than the lavish displays of grave goods seen earlier, the artefacts found in the cremation burials are usually personal ornaments, such as bronze pins and earrings. It is likely that many urn burials were covered by low mounds, although they have generally not survived ploughing.

At Telgte, near Münster in northwestern Germany, excavation of a 2-hectare (5-acre) area revealed 131 cremations. Many were surrounded by small, ditched enclosures. Some of the enclosures were round or oval, but 35 of them had a 'keyhole' shape in which the round end circled the burial pit but the enclosure extended outwards on one side, usually on a northwest–southeast axis. Some Telgte keyhole graves had structures built over them. Perhaps this was a way of marking the distinction of the deceased during and after the burial ceremony.

The practice in Scandinavia of marking the outline of a cremation burial with a 'ship setting' of standing stones has already been mentioned. It is an open question, however, whether these were then covered by a cairn or mound or whether they were meant to be seen openly. At Lugnaro in western Sweden, a ship setting about 8 metres (26 ft) long was covered by a mound. Inside were urns with the cremated remains of four individuals. One urn contained both human and sheep bones, a singed piece of wool cloth that did not get consumed by the fire and a dagger, tweezers and awl made from bronze.

Rituals, water and performance

With the spiritual realm already well embedded in the traditions of the Barbarian World, the ceremonialization of beliefs and relationships saw further elaboration in the second millennium BC. We have already seen how the construction of major burial monuments was part of this activity, although the other side of it was how these tombs were also designed to display wealth and status. Ritual life in Bronze Age Europe involved continued construction of monuments that formed focal points in ceremonial landscapes and the deposition of vast quantities of costly artefacts, mainly of bronze, in wet places such as swamps, bogs and rivers. In many respects, the advent of bronze metallurgy was not only a technological leap forward but also a completely new medium for consecrating offerings made to propitiate deities. It would be as if a modern cult were to hurl perfectly good smartphones into a lake.

Stone Age monuments such as Stonehenge continued in use well into the second millennium BC, and as seen above, hundreds of individual burial monuments were added to the surrounding ritual landscape. Timber also continued in use to make henges. At Holme-next-the-Sea in eastern England, an oval arrangement of 55 posts that were cut during the spring or early summer of 2049 BC was discovered in the intertidal zone. It appears to have been an Early Bronze Age ceremonial monument, dubbed 'Seahenge'.[14] Seahenge was relatively small, about 6.8 metres (22 ft) across, but its most impressive element was the huge stump of an oak tree that was cut or died in 2050 BC, overturned at its centre. What might have been the meaning of the stump, and what was the significance of the shoreline location of Seahenge?

During the second millennium BC, it seems that just about every wet location across the Barbarian World had the potential to be a site for offerings. For example, around 1350 BC, an immense timber structure was constructed in eastern England at Flag Fen, near the town of Peterborough and not far from the newly discovered settlement at Must Farm mentioned above.[15] At least 80,000 trees were cut down and their trunks sharpened into points to build five long rows of pilings that ran for over 1 kilometre (3,000 ft) across a swamp out to a small clay island. Many of these trees were oaks, not natural to the wetland environment, so they had to be brought from a distance. The exterior piles served as a sort of retaining system for the earth and timber fill between them that provided a relatively dry route across the swamp. Tree-ring dates indicate that the trees were cut between 1365 and 967 BC, suggesting that the structure was maintained and repaired over about 400 years.

At the deepest part of the swamp, the causeway was widened to form a platform by placing timbers across yet more pilings. From this platform, wooden, ceramic and metal objects, many

Holme Timber Circle, aka 'Seahenge'. The plank to the left of the central tree stump is from a 19-century shipwreck.

deliberately broken, were thrown into the swamp. Metal finds included swords, spearheads, earrings, pins and brooches. Mysterious small white stones were also gathered and thrown into the swamp. Deposits of metal items are also found along the causeway itself, but only on its southern side.

Rock art

Practices that emerged in the preceding millennia, especially the decoration of megalithic tombs, continued in traditions of rock art that flourished in parts of northern and western Europe during the Bronze Age.[16] The term 'rock art' means literally that: exposed outcrops decorated with images of people, objects and symbols that were pecked, ground and chiselled into the smooth surface of the rock. Major regional manifestations of rock art during the Bronze Age are found in Scandinavia and in the southern Alps.

The rocky Bohuslän region lies along the west coast of Sweden facing the North Sea. Along with central and southern Sweden and adjacent parts of Norway and Denmark, Bohuslän contains the greatest concentration of Nordic Bronze Age rock art. The Tanum area north of Gothenburg is the rock art capital of Bohuslän. Several hundred distinct outcrops have engravings, while hundreds more lie buried under moss and soil. The smooth, flat surfaces made marvellous canvases on which the carvers could kneel or lie while doing their work. When Bronze Age artists made them during the second millennium BC the Bohuslän engravings were close to the shoreline, but by the twenty-first century they had risen to 25–30 metres (80–100 ft) above sea level because the Swedish peninsula continues to rebound after being pushed down by ice over ten millennia ago.

Many outcrops have complex displays that are trying to tell us something about the social and spiritual lives of the societies that produced them. Ships with raised prows and sterns, often carrying people, are the most abundant image, and thousands have been recorded. Other people are shown bearing weapons, playing bronze trumpets, pushing ploughs, riding chariots drawn by oxen and having sex (many of the figures are unequivocally male). Animals include cattle, horses, deer, aquatic birds, dogs and wolves. Abstract images include cup marks (simple hemispherical pits), suns and spirals. Tracings of feet and hands are also common.

Many Scandinavian rock engravings were planned compositions, while some seem more haphazard or additive. Combat, rituals, processions, ploughing, hunting and seafaring would have been familiar elements of life in the Bronze Age, but we do not know what the carvings were trying to communicate. Were the carvings locations or backdrops for activities such as initiations or celebrations? Did the capture of these images hold deeper significance in cosmology, magic and beliefs? What did they say about the relationship between the world of the living and the world of myths and deities? Or were the carvings simply a Bronze Age version of Pinterest?

The other region that contains a concentration of Bronze Age rock art lies in the southwestern Alps of northwest Italy and southeast France. Here lie two exemplary sites: Mont Bego in the French Maritime Alps and Val Camonica in Lombardy. At both places, and several other important localities, the tradition of rock carving began during the Stone Age and continued through the first millennium BC, but it flourished spectacularly during the Bronze Age.

The rock here is softer than Scandinavian granite, and the schist and sandstone outcrops could be chiselled with pointed metal or stone tools to produce many thousands of images. At Mont Bego, nearly 100,000 carvings are known, while at Val Camonica the number exceeds 200,000. Weapons and tools are common motifs at both sites, reflecting both the functional and symbolic significance of these objects. Matching them to dated finds of actual tools and weapons from archaeological sites has permitted the dating of the carvings. In the Mont Bego carvings, another common image is horned oxen, sometimes two or four, pulling a plough. At Val Camonica, some carvings appear to show houses, stables or workshops with pitched roofs. Others have been interpreted as schematic maps of fields and dwellings.

Most parts of the Barbarian World were not so blessed with such massive rock outcrops that lent themselves to chiselling and engraving. A few cupmarks are all that might be expected in most places, although at some tombs like Kivik in southern Sweden, flat stone slabs were decorated in the same way as the boulders.[17] We can only imagine, however, how perishable materials such as wood were used for creating displays of people, weapons, tools and ships. Through the images on rock we get a glimpse of ritualized practices and performances that must have been ingrained in life during the second millennium BC.

Irish gold

A visitor to the National Museum of Ireland on Kildare Street in Dublin has an opportunity to see some of the most spectacular prehistoric gold objects from anywhere in the world.[18] Even more remarkable is the fact that these come not from a literate civilization but from the Bronze Age in Ireland, between about 2200 and 800 BC.[19] Not only is the quantity of gold in the museum cases impressive, but the craftsmanship demonstrated in the fabrication of these artefacts also represents mastery of a challenging material.

The working of gold during the Bronze Age in Ireland has two peaks, one at the beginning during the transition from the Stone

Bronze Age rock carvings at Tanum, southwest Sweden, highlighted in red paint, showing male warriors fighting on a boat.

Age to the use of metals, and the second at the end, just before the appearance of iron. During the Early Bronze Age, between about 2200 and 1800 BC, Irish goldsmiths hammered gold into thin sheets and then shaped it into flat objects. The most impressive of these are the lunulae, or crescent-shaped neck ornaments so named because of their resemblance to a waxing moon. Over eighty have been found in Ireland. The pointed ends of the lunulae are often bent at an angle to the plane of the gold sheet to form terminals, while their surface is often covered with fine geometric engraving that continues motifs seen on Stone Age pottery or bone. Many have rippled surfaces from having been rolled or folded. Lunulae were presumably worn suspended from the neck. Other Early Bronze Age sheet-gold forms include round plaques that may have been worn on clothing, as well as earrings.

It was long assumed that the source of the early Irish gold was in Ireland. Stream deposits in the mountains of eastern Ireland were often mentioned as likely sources. Recently, however, a research group led by Christopher Standish of the University of Southampton in England has studied trace elements in the thin gold sheet used to make artefacts like lunulae and discs.[20] Their surprising discovery was that the elemental composition of these artefacts did not match any known Irish gold sources. Thus, two possibilities emerge. The first is that the gold came from an unknown Irish gold source or one that has been exhausted. The second, which is more straightforward, is that the gold came from somewhere else. In Standish's study, Cornwall in southwestern England has emerged as a likely source. Thus it seems that gold from Cornwall was being traded to Ireland early in the second millennium BC in exchange for copper from southwestern Ireland and perhaps other resources. This copper, in turn, would have fed the demand for copper to alloy with Cornish tin and satisfy the desire for bronze in Britain and beyond. Despite the fact that there were local gold sources, Irish Bronze Age elites could point towards their access to a material from a distant source as a sign of their prestige. They needed to make the imported material go as far as possible, hence it was hammered wafer-thin.

Later in the second millennium BC, Irish goldworking went into decline only to re-emerge with new techniques around 1000 BC. In addition to gold sheet, now hammered so thin it would be called foil, solid objects of cast, shaped and twisted gold were made. Thus they are much more three-dimensional than the earlier flat objects. Bracelets and collars of twisted gold known as torcs are the most prominent, but some of the most interesting are thick and smooth curved objects with round ends given the speculative name of 'dress fasteners'. Late Bronze Age gold objects are often found in deposits or hoards, where they were placed for ritual reasons. In marshy ground along a lake at Mooghaun in Co. Clare, a hoard found in 1854 contained over 150 gold artefacts, mainly bracelets but also gold collars and neck rings, which weighed over 5 kilograms (11 lb).

In 1932, young Patrick Nolan was hunting in a part of Co. Clare known as the Burren, which today is a strange, denuded limestone landscape but which in prehistoric times had much more vegetation.[21] A rabbit ran into a fissure in the limestone. Patrick looked into the hole to find it, and instead of a rabbit he pulled out a spectacular gold collar measuring about 31 centimetres (1 ft) at its widest point. Today, the Gleninsheen Gorget, as it is known, is one of the most iconic Irish Late Bronze Age gold artefacts. Like the earlier lunulae, it is made from sheet gold in a crescent shape, only now it has thick ribs along its arc, separated by fine beaded decoration made by careful hammering. The terminals of the Gleninsheen Gorget are formed from round, concave pieces of ornamented sheet gold stitched to the crescent with gold wire. Gorgets like the one from Gleninsheen were composite artefacts formed from multiple gold sheets decorated and assembled with a remarkable level of detail and care.

During the second explosion of Irish goldworking, it seems likely that gold from local sources came into greater prominence, given the vast amount needed to produce massive torcs, bracelets, gorgets and other gold objects. Identifying the sources is still a challenge, however, and the recovery of gold particles from deposits in streams would have been a tedious and time-consuming process. Another question is the role that this extensive gold production played in arrangements of wealth, status and prestige in Irish Bronze Age society. Might such valuable objects have been gifts between chiefs to cement alliances? Why were they then buried in hoards or in hiding places? These questions, along with many others about Bronze Age Europe, await answers.

The Barbarian World in 800 BC

By the beginning of the first millennium BC, the general outlines of the Barbarian World that are of interest because of their eventual interactions with Mediterranean civilizations were falling into place. Bronze was in widespread use for weapons, tools and ornaments, often in massive forms that enabled its conspicuous display. Copper mines such as Mount Gabriel in Ireland, Great Orme in Wales and the Mitterberg in Austria fed the demand for raw material. Metalsmiths were masters of alloying, casting and finishing bronze in ever more elaborate forms. In addition, in particular areas like Ireland, goldworking techniques became especially advanced.

Bronze Age agriculture was a mature, integrated system of field cultivation and animal use, using the same primary domesticated plants and animals as before. Oxen were widely used for ploughing and pulling wagons. House forms varied from place to place, but in much of northern Europe a three-aisled longhouse was a standard domestic form. In some places, farmsteads were enclosed by ditches, while elsewhere they were open.

At the beginning of the second millennium BC, burial under mounds was a widespread burial rite, but by the beginning of the first millennium it was only found in Scandinavia, where huge mounds were built on ridgelines in Denmark and southern Sweden. Elsewhere, cremation was again the preferred means of disposing of the dead, often in large, flat cemeteries with the bones placed in urns along with bronze ornaments.

Trade networks flourished across the Barbarian World. First, tin and copper to make bronze needed to be brought together from separate sources, often necessitating transport of raw materials across bodies of water. Scrap bronze from broken and worn-out

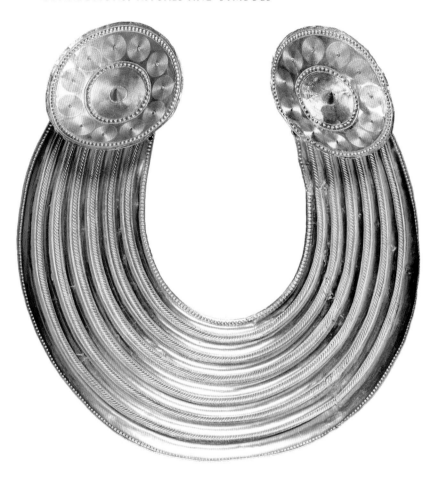

The Gleninsheen Gorget, a masterwork of Irish Late Bronze Age goldwork.

tools was melted down and reworked. Finely made bronze objects often wound up in abundance in places such as Denmark that utterly lacked both tin and copper, indicating the acquisitiveness of the inhabitants of such areas. Boatbuilding technology developed to meet the requirements for bulk transport of materials and products, as well as of people.

Finally, after some glimmers during previous millennia, we see the beginnings of ceremonial and spiritual life focused on making offerings by depositing costly items in wet places like bogs, ponds and rivers. Localities like Flag Fen became sites of sustained offering activity over several centuries. Stonehenge continued to be a place of congregation, and artefacts like the Nebra Disc reflect a keen interest in celestial bodies. Rock art across Scandinavia and in the Alps provided yet another medium for the expression of ideology and cosmology.

THREE

TRADE, SALT, GREEKS AND WEALTH

Early in the first millennium BC, the Barbarian World experienced local and regional bursts of economic and social complexity. Many of the themes running through this book continue to intersect and converge, and between about 800 and 400 BC we see the elaboration of trade networks and mortuary ceremonialism on a regional scale. Although this period is referred to as the early part of the Iron Age, the introduction of iron and its use for tools and implements took place gradually. As with the transition from the Stone Age to the Bronze Age, the transition from the Bronze Age to the Iron Age was seamless, especially from the perspective of people who lived through it.

The coming of iron

Iron had already started coming into use, but at first without major economic importance, during the final centuries of the Bronze Age. Unlike bronze, which requires that two metals from different sources be alloyed, iron ore is very widely distributed in Europe. A source was probably very close to most centres of population from the Atlantic to the Urals. This could be high-grade ore from montane regions or low-grade bog ore or limonite from sedimentary zones. Either could be concentrated through smelting to produce similar intermediate products that could be forged and shaped into all sorts of useful items.

The smelting of iron requires a large amount of fuel, usually charcoal, and enough air to heat the charcoal and ore mix to produce a 'bloom'. At first this was done in pits, but techniques later improved to use clay furnaces above the ground. Temperatures reached 2000–2400°C (1100–1300°F), substantially higher than needed to smelt copper. After sufficient heating, the slag waste would settle to the bottom of the furnace, leaving the bloom to be extracted and worked further by heating and hammering.

Although iron is more ubiquitous than copper and tin, its production nonetheless required considerable skill to achieve the high temperatures needed for smelting, refining the bloom and forging the metal into useful products. New techniques had to be learned and perfected. Casting, the principal method of the Bronze Age, was not especially useful for early iron. Forging and blacksmithing came to be important and valued skills.

The advantage of iron over bronze is that it is exceptionally durable and can keep a sharp edge. Swords made from iron would break only under tremendous impact, and their edges could be repeatedly sharpened. Since it was less expensive to produce, useful implements such as kettles, hooks and shears could be made. Rivets and nails became available for fastening wood, simplifying joinery and allowing heavy items to be suspended. It took a while before these useful applications of the new metal were figured out, but centres of iron production soon sprang up across the Barbarian World.

One such centre was at Stična in modern Slovenia.[1] Here, local high-quality iron ore was smelted, forged and transported throughout the eastern Alps and northern Italy. As a result, considerable wealth flowed into Stična, reflected in the contents of thousands of nearby burials.

Yet iron did not replace bronze, especially for luxury goods. Many finely made objects, such as elaborately decorated buckets, found in the Stična graves were made from bronze. Throughout later prehistory, bronze was the primary metal for making really nice things, whereas iron was the pragmatic choice for making tools that needed to be cheap and abundant or tough and sharp. Iron goods were meant to be used.

Antenna-hilted dagger with iron blade from Hallstatt, Austria, in the Natural History Museum, Vienna.

The traditional periodization for the end of the Bronze Age and the beginning of the Iron Age uses the term Hallstatt, which, as we will see below, is the name of an important site in Austria. The Hallstatt period is divided into four parts, A to D, with the first two being the final stages of the Bronze Age characterized by cremation burials and the last two being the first stages of the Iron Age. Hallstatt stages are primarily markers for archaeological specialists, but the term crops up often in descriptions of the period between 800 and 400 BC. It is often applied to the strongly differentiated societies of the seventh, sixth and fifth centuries BC in central Europe.

Who were the Celts?

'Were the people who lived at the sites you study . . . Celts?' I have been often asked this question when talking about the Stone Age settlements that I investigate in Poland. I have to answer, 'No, my farmers lived several thousand years before people who could have been called Celts lived in Europe.' The passive phrase 'could have been called' is important. No one in the southern or western part of temperate Europe during the final millennium BC would have recognized the name 'Celt'. Celts are only what other people called them, both in the past and in more recent times. Nonetheless, they were real people, and during the period discussed in this chapter we begin to see common traits that mark a Celtic *tradition* in language and decorative style running through the later prehistory of Germany, France and the British Isles.

Peoples known as Celts have deep archaeological roots in late Bronze Age central Europe, before 800 BC. This tradition continues through Hallstatt chiefdoms of west-central Europe between 600 and 450 BC, in which trade with Greek merchants produced remarkable demonstrations of status and wealth. We will explore this relationship in greater detail below. Although these trading contacts abated around 450 BC, Celts were now known to the Mediterranean world. Some groups moved south, into the Balkans and Italy, even as far as Anatolia. The Celtic tradition then continued into the remarkable La Tène art style of the final centuries BC that will be described in the next chapter and persists today in the native languages of Ireland, Scotland and Brittany and the cultural identities that accompany them.

Around 500 BC, the Greek author Hecataeus of Miletus wrote about people he called *Keltoi*, with specific reference to the peoples from northern Europe who had migrated into the southern Balkans, Greece and even Anatolia, and whom the Greeks had encountered at their trading colony of Massalia. Scholars call words like *Keltoi* or Celts an ethnonym, meaning an externally applied collective name given to a group of people to distinguish them from their neighbours. With time, this term came to be applied to barbarian aggressors with whom the Greeks and later the Romans had contact during the second half of the first millennium BC, when Celtic bands penetrated into the Balkans and Italy, sacking Rome in 390 BC.

From writings of classical authors such as Posidonius and later Caesar and Tacitus, we know something of Celtic society. Various traits were ascribed to Celts, most notably fighting and drinking. They had oral traditions that were managed by priests (later identified as 'druids'), bards and poets. A warrior elite served the leaders, whose success in battle was a claim to power and authority. Craft specialists became expert in working materials such as bronze, gold and coral, which also took on spiritual significance. Feasting cemented relations among the elite. An important Celtic institution was the practice of clientship. Noble patrons provided clients with protection and prestige while obtaining support and service in return.

Many books have been written on the barbarians known as Celts,[2] but this term will not appear much in the remainder of this book. One reason is that the prehistoric Celts represent only some of the barbarians of temperate Europe, and the distinction between them and contemporaneous inhabitants of temperate Europe is largely imposed by the outsiders. A major theme of this book is the 'diversity in uniformity' of later prehistoric Europe, and separating Celts from other barbarian peoples introduces a discordant note. The major reason for not focusing more on Celts, however, is that another ethnonym is being used throughout this book, namely 'the Barbarian World', which includes both peoples known as Celts and all the other pre-literate societies of temperate Europe.

Waterlogged lakeside villages in northern Poland

Many parts of northern Poland are lakelands in which Ice Age glaciers left shallow depressions and valleys that filled with water. These were attractive places for settlement in prehistoric times as they are today, because the surrounding dryland areas are covered with fertile soils and the streams that connected these lakes enabled easy travel by watercraft. One such lake is Lake Biskupin, located about 60 kilometres (40 mi.) north of the city of Poznań. On a soggy peninsula jutting into the lake, a remarkable fortified Iron Age settlement was discovered in 1933.[3]

A local schoolteacher, Walenty Szwajcer, had read about the Swiss Lake Dwellings. One day, he noticed waterlogged timbers protruding from the boggy soil by the lake, and he imagined that he had found their Polish equivalent. He reported his discovery to the

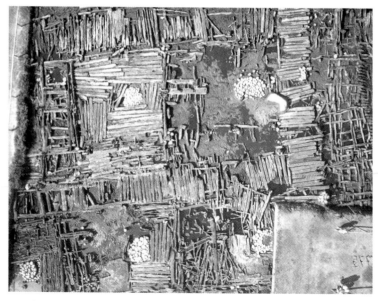

Aerial photo of the 1930s excavations at Biskupin, Poland, taken from a Polish Army observation balloon.

Archaeological Museum in Poznań, where the news made its way to Józef Kostrzewski (1885–1968), one of the founders of modern archaeology in Poland. Kostrzewski recognized the importance of the find, and the following summer, he began excavations.

Kostrzewski and his team of assistants and workmen systematically uncovered the tangle of waterlogged timbers. Eventually, outlines of houses and streets began to emerge. The houses were built in long rows, with shared walls between them, separated by streets paved with oak logs. Each of over 100 houses was similar to the others, measuring about 8 by 9 metres (26 × 30 ft). They consisted of a large central room with a stone hearth, entered through an antechamber used for storage.

Surrounding the settlement was a rampart of timber boxes filled with earth and stones. It enclosed an oval area approximately 160 metres (525 ft) wide and 200 metres (660 ft) long and is estimated to have been 5–6 metres (16–20 ft) high. Sharpened wooden stakes along the shore of the lake on three sides of the site served as a breakwater to protect the rampart from erosion as well as a deterrent to enemies trying to launch a waterborne attack. A main gate permitted access to the interior street system. The internal organization of the streets and houses suggests that planning went into the layout of the settlement before it was built.

Kostrzewski employed novel techniques for the time.[4] He enlisted the Polish Army to fly an observation Zeppelin over the excavations to obtain photographs taken vertically to show the settlement layout, while Polish Navy divers explored the lake bottom. Careful attention was paid to the recovery and analysis of animal bones and plant remains. Kostrzewski organized an extensive publicity campaign in the press. His excavations were interrupted by the Second World War, during which further investigation was carried out by the ss-Ahnenerbe (see Chapter Six). After the war, Kostrzewski's pupils continued research at Biskupin. Although major excavations ended in the 1970s, research on the site continues today.

Analysis of plant remains and animal bones revealed that the inhabitants of Biskupin were farmers who grew millet, wheat, barley, rye and beans and kept pigs for meat and cattle for meat and milk. A big question is how many people lived at Biskupin. Some estimates are in the order of 700 to 1,000 people, although those seem high. Nonetheless, Biskupin clearly represented a concentration of several hundred people that made heavy demands on the surrounding fields, pastures and forests. Cattle were also used to pull wagons and ploughs, since wooden wheels and plough-shares were found among the timbers.

Early radiocarbon dates indicated that Biskupin was occupied between 700 and 600 BC, but more accurate dating has been provided by tree-ring dating of the waterlogged timbers.[5] Most of the trees used in the construction of Biskupin were cut between 747 and 722 BC. Almost half of them were felled during the winter of 738–737 BC. Although the actual duration of the settlement is unclear, there was at least one major episode of rebuilding after a fire. Nonetheless, the settlement was abandoned in the final decade of the eighth century BC, around 708 BC.

We also now know that Biskupin was not unique.[6] Many other lakes in the region also had fortified sites around roughly the same time. Sobiejuchy lies 14 kilometres (9 mi.) north of Biskupin, on an isthmus between two lakes that was probably an island 2,700 years ago. Although it covers a larger area, the internal organization of Sobiejuchy is very different to Biskupin, in that its houses are long and narrow and are not as densely packed. Other sites, like Smuszewo and Izdebno, have the same sort of packed layout as Biskupin. The fact that there were two flavours of settlement plan in this small area highlights the fact that the Barbarian World was far from homogeneous.

We do not know why Biskupin and nearby sites were abandoned, apparently after only a few decades. The climate did turn a bit moister at this time, so rising lake levels have been suggested. Attacks and raids by marauders have also been proposed, and the massive ramparts indicate that defence was a major concern. Perhaps the cause of their collapse was internal. Their construction would have required so much timber that acres of forest needed to be felled, although that area would have been put to good use for fields and pastures. Several hundred people packed into confined spaces also would have posed a problem. Conflicts between

Reconstruction of rampart and gate at Biskupin, Poland. Note the sharpened posts outside the rampart, which served as a breakwater and a defensive feature.

individuals and families would have been difficult to resolve, and in the end it may have been that internal stresses caused the downfall of Biskupin and its neighbours.

Salt becomes wealth

Salt was an essential commodity for ancient societies in which the supply of meat and fish exceeded the ability of people to consume it all at one sitting. By the beginning of the first millennium BC, communities throughout Europe living near natural sources of salt had figured out how to trade it to other communities that were not so fortunate. This required the ability to produce salt on an industrial scale by mining salt deposits or evaporating brine or seawater; the ability to pack it densely into containers for transport; access to transportation systems capable of hauling heavy loads, using oxcarts and watercraft; and the ability of the consumers to pay in metal goods, crops, furs and anything else they could grow or make.

The more salt a community could produce, the more goods flowed back to it. By the time the flow of traded goods reached back to the source, their value had been channelled into luxury items rather than mundane commodities. The result was that some communities became fantastically wealthy. Thus began a golden age for the salt miners of central Europe. Salt evaporation from seawater or brine was limited by the fact that it was a batch process, and there were natural limits on its volume. Evaporation operations appear to have served local demand. Mining the giant salt domes of central Europe, on the other hand, was limited only by the supply of labour and how fast salt could be carried out of the ground and shipped.

One salt-rich community was found at Hallstatt in the Austrian Alps, already mentioned above as having given its name to this general period. During the middle of the first millennium BC, Hallstatt came to sit at the top of an economic system in which mined salt was traded to farming hamlets in a wide area of central Europe and the northern part of the Mediterranean basin in exchange for all sorts of luxury goods. Thanks to nearly two centuries of archaeological investigation, we know quite a bit about the mining community at Hallstatt.

Hallstatt's miners and their graves

The Austrian Alps south of Salzburg (the clue is the name, since *Salz* is German for salt) tower over the valley of the Salzach river (again, the name) and enclose lake basins in their depths. The modern town of Hallstatt (again, the name is a clue, as *Hall-* is an older German root meaning salt) is reached over winding roads through mountain passes which descend into the basin of a deep lake surrounded by steep mountainsides. Between two slopes that overlook the town clinging to the narrow lakeshore, a valley, the Salzbergtal, leads back into the mountains. In the valley lie prehistoric salt mines and an Iron Age cemetery that make Hallstatt one of the most important sites for understanding how wealth was accumulated during the first millennium BC.[7]

At Hallstatt, ancient miners followed veins of nearly pure rock salt by sinking shafts that angled down from the mountainside, reaching depths of nearly 330 metres (1,100 ft). The veins are about

5 metres (16 ft) thick, and ladders made from notched tree trunks were used to reach higher spots. Using bronze picks, miners cut a vertical groove in the salt face, then two curving grooves to each side. The two lobes of salt thus formed were prised off and carried out to the surface, while loose salt was scooped up and shovelled into cowhide backpacks with wooden frames.[8] Miners' backpacks had a clever but simple feature, a wooden rod sticking up from one side. When the carrier reached the collection point, he or she simply bent over and pulled the rod, which tipped the bag forward and allowed the salt to spill out.

The most common traces of human activity inside the Hallstatt mountain are burnt pieces of wood used by miners as torches and heating fires. Miners also left clothing made from wool and linen, along with leather shoes and hats. They were simply made. For example, a cone-shaped cap is stitched together from triangles of hide with the hairy side on the interior for warmth.

Mining was dangerous, and despite shoring, cave-ins took their toll. In 1734, the corpse of an accident victim was found inside the mountain, preserved in the salt. His clothes and shoes, as well as the circumstances of the find, made it clear that he was a prehistoric miner. When he was found, the concern of the eighteenth-century miners was whether or not he was a Christian. They decided that he probably was not, so his corpse was buried in unconsecrated ground outside the parish cemetery, where pagans and suicides were interred. Removed from the salt, the body decayed quickly. How many more corpses of prehistoric miners are still entombed in the mountain?

The wealth derived from salt is reflected in the cemetery a short distance down the Salzbergtal from the mine entrances. Since the middle of the nineteenth century, over 1,100 prehistoric graves have been found, including both cremations and skeleton burials, while many more were probably destroyed by later mining. The Hallstatt burials contain bronze and iron swords and daggers, bronze bowls and cauldrons, helmets and ornaments of glass, amber and metal. Exotic materials testify to the extent of the network that brought these goods to Hallstatt. For example, one sword handle was made from ivory with amber inlays. It is

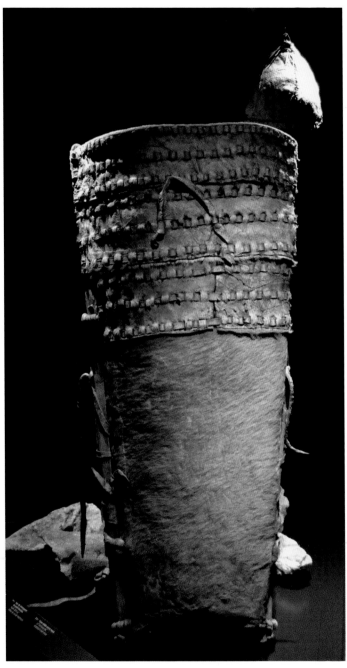

Bronze Age backpack for carrying salt from the Hallstatt mine; presumably similar equipment was used during the Iron Age.

not known whether the ivory came from Africa or Asia, but the fact that it wound up on a hillside in central Europe in the middle of the first millennium BC testifies to connections between the Barbarian World and lands far beyond.

We do not know where the Hallstatt miners lived, for no settlement has yet been found. Analysis of the graves suggests that it was a normal Iron Age community composed of family households rather than a specialized mining settlement with a disproportionate number of men. Women and children as well as men worked in the mines. Examination of female skeletons indicated that they often carried heavy loads over one shoulder, so perhaps it was they who used the backpacks described above.

Barbarians meet the Greeks

Until now, the Mediterranean World has hovered outside the picture to the south. During the first millennium BC, Greek civilization was reaching its zenith. Greek city states looked beyond the Aegean for new opportunities for power and wealth. The epic tales of Jason and Odysseus were anchored in a seafaring tradition, and Greeks set out west across the Mediterranean and north into the Black Sea basin to establish trading posts. Their goal was not to conquer indigenous peoples and colonize territory but rather to obtain products and raw materials in exchange for the output of Greek workshops and vineyards. Over time, these emporia became embedded in local economies and attracted settlers from the Greek homeland, which brought Greeks into contact with the Barbarian World.

Initial forays led Greeks to the Adriatic, where traders from Corinth established a colony on Corfu. Then they reached southern Italy and Sicily, which over time developed into a cluster of Greek colonies collectively known as Magna Graecia, in which the city state of Syracuse became the largest *polis* in the Greek world. Colonists from Thera (Santorini) crossed the Mediterranean to set up shop in Cyrene in North Africa. It was when the Greeks reached further north, through the Hellespont into the Black Sea basin, and north from Magna Graecia to the southern coast of

France, that they had their most important contacts with the Barbarian World. These contacts not only were profitable for the Greek colonists but they also transformed barbarian societies not just at the site of the colony but far inland.

Greeks trigger a gilded age in central Europe

One such colony, named Massalia, lay at the mouth of the Rhône river on the Mediterranean coast of France. The history of Massalia (the Greek spelling, also encountered in the Latin spelling, Massilia, which became the modern Marseilles) really begins at the city state of Phocaea (modern Foça) in western Turkey. Colonists from Phocaea set out westward to found a trading colony at the mouth of the Rhône around 600 BC. A marriage between a prominent Greek and the daughter of a local chief is said to have sealed the deal to enable the Greeks to set up their trading post.

Massalia's location was propitious, for the Rhône, its tributary the Saône and the Saône's tributary the Doubs lead nearly 950 kilometres (600 mi.) north into the heart of west-central Europe. At its headwaters, the Rhône–Saône–Doubs system connects overland to the headwaters of the Seine, the Rhine and the Loire, providing a direct route from the Mediterranean to the North Sea and Atlantic coast. Barbarian communities throughout much of western Europe soon felt the effects of the Greek presence at Massalia.

What the Greeks could offer the central European elites were finely crafted products of the workshops of Magna Graecia and wine, as well as objects from the Greek homeland itself. Etruscan products from northern Italy also made their way to Massalia or in some cases over the Alps. Eventually, Massalia's own workshops and vineyards began to produce goods for this trade. From Massalia, wine and luxury goods made their way north, possibly through chains of middlemen or Massaliote agents, until they made their way to southern Germany and eastern France.

Trade with the Greeks in Massalia made some people in central Europe very wealthy. This wealth, in turn, was transformed into status and prestige, resulting in very elaborate settlements and lavish burials. While we do not completely understand the microeconomic factors that led to this sudden concentration of wealth and status, the effect was the display, sometimes seemingly ostentatious, of material trappings of prestige in life and in death. The strongholds and burials of the Iron Age elites of central Europe have a very *nouveau riche* aspect to them. If these people were alive today, we would read about them in the *Daily Mail* or *People* magazine.

These acquisitive elites of central Europe fashioned hilltop locations into fortified compounds across southern Germany and into eastern France. Here they displayed their status to the surrounding countryside. These compounds are parts of complex settlements at which hundreds, perhaps even thousands, of people lived, presumably retainers of the local chief and his family. About a dozen sites stand out, bearing the fanciful name of 'princely seats' (*Fürstensitze* in German). Recent research has led to new insights about the organization of these settlements, the activities that went on there, and their hinterlands.

Mont Lassois

About 200 kilometres (125 mi.) southeast of Paris in Burgundy, Mont Lassois overlooks the village of Vix along the Seine river. Its higher end is a broad plateau with a surface of about 5 hectares (2 acres). This plateau was already the site of a Bronze Age fortified settlement, but after a hiatus of three centuries it was redeveloped into a densely occupied citadel in use between 620 and 450 BC.

Recent geophysical survey of the plateau has yielded a detailed picture of the organization of the settlement on Mont Lassois.[9] An arterial 'Main Street' ran almost the length of the plateau from north to south. On either side were neighbourhoods defined by ditches and palisades which contained buildings of various sizes, from small to monumental. The impression is of a well-planned, structured community, surrounded by timber and stone ramparts.

In one of the compounds two very large buildings were built between 530/20 and 480/50 BC. The larger one measures 35 by 22 metres (115 × 72 ft), with an interior area of over 500 square metres

(5,000 sq. ft), while the smaller is 25 by 14 metres (82 × 46 ft). They are expertly laid out and consist of three sections: an entrance hall, a main hall and a large curving apse that gives them distinctive church-like plans. The height of the larger building is estimated at about 15 metres (50 ft), making it truly immense. At one point it was destroyed by fire and rebuilt. Sitting on top of the plateau, it was probably visible for miles around. The function of these large apsidal buildings is unclear. Were they elite residences, locations of rituals or communal meeting houses? Perhaps they served several different functions.

The Heuneburg

Perhaps the most celebrated princely site overlooks the Danube in southwestern Germany. The Heuneburg lies on a hilltop that began to be fortified late in the Bronze Age as the site of a small village, which was then abandoned. Around 650 BC, intense building activity began, leading to the enclosure of 3.3 hectares (8 acres). During the next two centuries, walls around the hilltop were destroyed and rebuilt at least ten times.

During an early reconfiguration of the Heuneburg ramparts, around 600 BC, a part of the wall was built from sun-dried clay bricks, up to a height of 4 metres (13 ft), on a base of limestone blocks.[10] Such construction is unique in central Europe, for the very good reason that it is unsuited to the wet, seasonal environment. Sun-dried mud bricks, after a while, simply dissolve, although those at the Heuneburg were conserved by frequent replastering. In the end, the burning of its wooden walkway, evidently by an attack, caused the destruction of the mud-brick wall.

The only plausible reason to build a Mediterranean-style wall in central Europe was that its patron wished to demonstrate familiarity with exotic practices from distant lands to enhance his prestige. Perhaps he had been to Massalia, seen similar walls, tried to copy them. Mud brick was probably a challenge to make and maintain. After the mud-brick wall was destroyed around 540–530 BC, the fortification was rebuilt using traditional methods of timber cribbing filled with stone.

Mont Lassois, Burgundy, France, seat of an Iron Age 'prince' with monumental structures, which overlooks the Vix tomb.

The mud-brick wall at the Heuneburg is a vivid demonstration of connections between the central European elites and the Mediterranean world. Imported objects found at the Heuneburg included Greek black-figure pottery and amphorae made in Provence, in the hinterland of Massalia, that presumably contained wine brought up the Rhône drainage. The central European elites in the sixth century BC were really into wine, and the Greeks were only too happy to indulge their tastes.

It was long thought that settlement at the Heuneburg was confined to the fortified hilltop. Since the early 1990s, investigations at the base of the hill and in the surrounding countryside revealed a fortified lower settlement surrounded by a ditch and rampart. It covered nearly 20 hectares (50 acres) and contained both houses and workshops for working bronze and weaving cloth. To level the uneven land, small terraces were constructed. Excavations revealed a massive gate into the lower settlement, constructed, like the wall of the hillfort above, of mud brick on a stone foundation. A bridge across the ditch led into the gate, which was designed to provide a monumental entrance. Wood from the bridge was dated to 590 BC using tree rings.[11]

Beyond the lower settlement was an agrarian landscape covering over 100 hectares (250 acres), with closely spaced farmsteads grouped into larger quarters. The quarters were divided by ditches, and the farmsteads were surrounded by rectangular palisades. Other elements of the surrounding landscape were burial mounds and small hamlets. Thus the Heuneburg did not sit alone but was the centre of an immense settlement complex. Population estimates run into several thousands. The complexity of the settlement, the evidence for craft production and specialization and the long-distance trade and high populations have led some to propose that these sites have an 'urban' quality and qualify as early cities. Monumental buildings and evidence for planning at Mont Lassois have also led to use of the term 'quasi-urban' in recent interpretations. Whether or not this proves to be the case, the Heuneburg and the other princely compounds are the residential and industrial part of the Hallstatt florescence.

Princely graves

The story of the Hallstatt elites of central Europe is not only about the fortified residences, however. Even more luminous elements of the archaeological landscape are the massive tumuli with single main burials in chambers packed full of luxury items.[12] The discovery in the late 1970s of an unrobbed burial of an Iron Age 'prince' at Hochdorf in southwestern Germany was a sensation. The mound that covered it had been overlooked not only by grave robbers but also by archaeologists until 1977.[13] The contents of the Hochdorf tomb make it perhaps the richest burial in central Europe.

The Hochdorf 'prince'

The burial mound at Hochdorf originally stood about 6 metres (20 ft) high, but erosion and ploughing reduced its height so much that it was scarcely visible. It is nearly 60 metres (200 ft) in diameter. Dug 2.5 metres (8 ft) below the original ground surface was a square burial chamber about 11 metres (36 ft) on each side. Inside the chamber were two wooden boxes, one inside the other, both made from oak, each covered with a timber roof. The inner box contained the burial and its grave goods. Space between the boxes was filled with stones, with more stones piled up over the roofs of the compartments, 50 metric tons (55 tons) in all. Unfortunately, this weight was too much for even the stout oak timbers, and they caved in. The good thing was that this allowed many perishable items in the tomb such as wood and textiles to become water-logged and preserved.

The man buried in the Hochdorf tomb was about forty years old and stood around 1.8 metres (6 ft) tall. He was wearing a conical birchbark hat, perhaps not as warm as the hide one from Hallstatt but still stylish, and a gold neck ring. A small bag on his chest contained a wooden comb, an iron razor, five amber beads and three iron fishhooks. His clothing and even his shoes were adorned with bands of hammered gold. Lying next to him was his bow and a quiver of arrows.

The man's body was lying on a bronze settee, like a sofa, draped with badger skins. On the back and sides of the settee are scenes of wagons and dancers, while its legs are bronze figures of women with raised arms. Wheels under their feet enabled it to be rolled. This remarkable piece of furniture has no known parallels in ancient Europe. At the foot of the settee is a bronze vessel decorated with three lions, made in a workshop in Magna Graecia. It could hold about 500 litres (110 gal.). Residue in the vessel was from a fermented honey beverage, probably drunk from a small gold bowl found inside the vessel. Drinking was clearly important, for nine drinking horns hung from the fabric-covered walls of the chamber.

On the opposite side of the chamber was a four-wheeled wagon with harnesses for two horses. Although sheathed in iron with sturdy ten-spoke wheels, the body of the wagon was so lightweight that it clearly was not intended for actual use, just for burial. More grave goods sat on its platform, including a set of bronze dishes, service for nine.

Despite the abundance of sumptuous grave goods, we know little about the man in the Hochdorf tomb, but we can make some

Detail of a lion on the rim of a bronze wine vessel at Hochdorf, Germany

inferences. We know his age and his height, and also that he was strongly built. He liked to hunt, fish, eat and drink. The number nine was also important, perhaps representing clients or retainers. The artefacts point towards a burial date of around 530–520 BC, which means he probably saw the mud-brick wall at the Heuneburg before it was destroyed. He and his people were rich, for the total weight of the gold around him is around 600 grams (21 oz), more than any other burial of this time. It is not difficult to infer that this was a very important individual in the upper tier of his society with access to considerable wealth.

The Lady of Vix

Along the Seine at Vix, in the shadow of Mont Lassois, lies a mound 38 metres (125 ft) in diameter. At its centre is a burial chamber, excavated in 1953, much like at Hochdorf.[14] Like Hochdorf, it contained a four-wheeled wagon, although the wheels of the wagon had been taken off and laid against the wall of the chamber.

On the wagon's platform lay the body of a woman. She was wearing a large gold neck ring with bulbous terminals decorated with tiny winged horses. Elsewhere in the tomb was a rich assortment of objects made from gold, amber and coral. Clearly a high-status person, she has become known as 'The Lady of Vix'.

Looming over everything in the tomb was a gigantic bronze vessel known as a krater. Standing around 1.64 metres (5 ft 4 in.) tall and weighing about 209 kilograms (460 lb), the Vix krater could hold around 1,100 litres (nearly 300 U.S. gallons or 240 imperial gallons). No doubt, the liquid it contained was wine, mixed with water, since that was the purpose of such large vessels in the Greek world. It was made in a workshop in the Greek colony of Magna Graecia, near the cities of Tarent (modern Taranto) and Sybaris (known archaeologically along the Gulf of Taranto) around 530 BC. Along with it were Attic black-figure drinking cups made about 520/515 BC.

The krater found in the Vix burial reminds us of the thirst for wine and prestige goods among the Hallstatt elites. It also shows that wine was consumed ostentatiously. The krater itself is an ostentation. Normally in the Greek world, these were made from pottery. Making a bronze vessel that weighed so much and then transporting it about 1,600 km (1,000 miles) over mountains and across rivers, or perhaps by sea to the mouth of the Rhône and then upstream from there, was all part of the show. So was its burial in the tomb. The Lady of Vix and her elite family were performing for their retainers to demonstrate their prestige and status. Were these the same elite who built the apsidal buildings on Mont Lassois? Very possibly.

A new tomb at Lavau

Traces of Hallstatt elites keep coming to light. In 2014, another princely burial was found at Lavau, near Troyes in France.[15] Since it looked like a natural low hill, it escaped looting, both in modern times and in antiquity. The mound at Lavau is 40 metres (130 ft) across. It concealed a collapsed burial chamber containing a single skeleton. Key elements of princely burials were present: a body

with gold jewellery; a vehicle, in this case a two-wheeled chariot; and copious amounts of wine-drinking and feasting paraphernalia, including Greek and Etruscan bronze vessels. The centrepiece was an immense bronze vat just under 1 metre (3 ft) in diameter decocircular handles, each bearing the head of the Greek river god Achelous. Achelous has a distinctive appearance with a squared-off beard, a moustache and the ears and horns of a bull. Inside this massive vessel was a Greek black-figure wine

Detail of a lion on the rim of a bronze wine vessel at Lavau, France.

pitcher called an *oinochoe*, with gold trim around the rim and base. Other bronze vessels and a silver sieve complete the wine-serving set.

The individual buried at Lavau had an immense gold ring, or torc, around the neck weighing 0.7 kilograms (1½ lb) and decorated with winged figures and prominent pear-shaped terminals. This form of personal ornament, along with amber beads, additional gold bracelets and coral garment ornaments, plus the absence of weapons, led to initial speculation that the person was a woman of high social standing, much like the Lady of Vix, about 65 kilometres (40 mi.) away. Subsequent testing, however, demonstrated that the individual in the Lavau tomb was a man.

The hill compounds and noble burials at the headwaters of major rivers like the Seine, Danube and Rhine show that the great portages between the major river systems of eastern central Europe were ideally suited for control of the trade along these corridors. The flow of goods in ancient times would be what transportation engineers today call 'intermodal', a combination of waterborne and overland transport. In the case of the Iron Age elites, the luxury goods they received from the Mediterranean world were one side of the story. The other involved the commodities moving south in exchange for them. Furs, beeswax, amber and perhaps slaves were acquired from the north, probably in exchange for fairly mundane agricultural and locally made craft products. These passed through the portages and were aggregated by the communities who lived there. As middlemen, they then could satisfy their taste for Mediterranean luxury goods.

Unfortunately, this arrangement did not last, and the conspicuous consumption in central Europe seems to have tailed off about 450 BC. Whether this reflects social turmoil or simply a reorientation of exchange networks is not known, but social complexity does not develop in a straight line. Since Mediterranean goods were essentially status symbols, perhaps the arc of popularity taken by such objects that we see today also prevailed in the past, and Greek goods ceased to be markers of power and wealth. Perhaps lower strata of society could also acquire them, so they were no longer signs of elite distinction. Whatever the reason, during the fifth century BC this chapter in the story of the Barbarian World ended.

Hillforts beyond the Channel

The decline in trade between the Greeks and central Europe did not signal the end of hillforts in other parts of western Europe, however. In the British Isles, particularly in Britain, the construction, occupation and development of central fortified sites continued apace. The hillforts of southern Britain did not depend on trade in exotic goods but rather appear to have been local responses to a need for centres of defence, crafts and authority by small, loosely integrated polities. Among the dozens of Iron Age hillforts, two of the best known are Maiden Castle in Dorset and Danebury in Hampshire.

Maiden Castle is a long, steep hill that had been the site of a ditched enclosure and long barrow during the Stone Age.[16] Around 500 BC a small hillfort was established on its eastern end. Over the next several centuries, it was expanded and strengthened, such that the contours of its slopes were dramatically transformed by three immense chalk ramparts and corresponding ditches. When they were first built, the white exposed chalk would have been visible from far away, extremely impressive and intimidating. In final form, Maiden Castle covered 47 hectares (116 acres).

The interior of Maiden Castle contained multiple roundhouses, typical for the British Iron Age, and four-post granaries. The latter are just over 2 metres (6 ft) square. They occur on Iron Age sites in southern Britain, and in a six-post form in other parts of the Barbarian World. Maiden Castle was reorganized several times, with a haphazard distribution of houses giving way to an organized settlement plan with arterial paths. Evidence for textile production and metalworking indicate that it was not a purely agrarian settlement or a temporary refuge.

The gateways are some of the most interesting features of Maiden Castle. Passages through the ramparts did not line up to provide a direct route into the interior but instead were offset, often by some distance, forcing an attacking force to move laterally through the intervening ditch and giving defenders an opportunity to rain arrows, spears and stones from above. While such complicated entrances are typical features of hillforts, the ramparts at Maiden Castle display them particularly vividly.

Danebury was excavated during the late twentieth century, and thus its interior and ramparts are known in considerable detail.[17] The hill on which it sits is not as steep as at Maiden Castle, and thus its defences are not as spectacular but dominate the surrounding landscape nonetheless. Its ramparts were expanded multiple times over several centuries of occupation, becoming progressively more elaborate and complex. Gates through them were strengthened with timber gatehouses which provided the complexity needed to slow down an attacking force. Bodies in mass graves suffered gruesome injuries or have been dismembered, presumably the outcome of an attack.

The interior of Danebury was occupied by roundhouses and four-post granaries as at Maiden Castle and other British hillforts. Settlement features have yielded nearly a quarter of a

Aerial photo of the Danebury hillfort in England showing multiple banks and ditches.

million animal bones. Of these about two-thirds were from sheep, clearly indicating the basis of the animal economy, used for meat, wool and milk. Cattle were also a substantial component of the economy, accounting for about a fifth of the bones, while pigs constituted about an eighth of the sample. Horses were used for riding, light pulling and as pack animals, although their remains in ritual deposits indicate that they were seen in a different category from the other livestock.

Hillforts like Maiden Castle and Danebury did not supplant the pattern of rural farmstead settlement that emerged in earlier millennia, however. They were centres for economic, ritual and commercial activity as well as refuges in times of conflict. Warfare, in the form of organized raiding parties and warrior bands, was constant, especially in southern England, during the second half of the first millennium BC.

The Barbarian World in 450 BC

Beginning about 800 BC, iron came into common use across the Barbarian World. It permitted the production of utilitarian objects on one hand and the manufacture of sharp weapons on the other, although it did not replace bronze for fine ornamental goods. Iron did not have the procurement and transport costs of copper and tin, and its production provided a new pathway to economic success for communities not yet so blessed.

The dominant theme across much of Europe during the middle of the first millennium BC was acquisition of desirable goods and vivid florescence of decentralized complexity. We can see this in the lakeside villages like Biskupin in northern Poland, the princely seats of acquisitive elites in central Europe and the industrial production of salt in exchange for luxury goods in the Austrian Alps.

Much of this activity occurred, either directly or indirectly, as a result of contacts with the Mediterranean world, particularly with Greek trading colonies. From one perspective, the Greeks took advantage of the desire by the inhabitants of temperate Europe for luxury goods to acquire the materials, products and slaves that they did not have in the Mediterranean zone. Another point of

view is that the Greeks were played like a cheap violin by barbarian elites, who sent them quantities of things that they had
in abundance for expensive exotic goods. Perhaps a little of each
was going on.

FOUR

ROMANS ENCOUNTER THE HIGH IRON AGE

T he final centuries BC saw further transformations of the Barbarian World. Political and social structures emerged that sponsored a remarkable artistic florescence known as the La Tène style and the eventual convergence of civic life at large fortified towns. In Britain, hillforts that developed during the middle of the first millennium BC became larger and populous. Across northern Europe, the use of wetlands and lakes for ritual purposes became even more elaborate, and humans were included among the sacrifices. Finally, in western Europe, the Barbarian World was dramatically changed by the intrusion of a powerful state: Rome.

It is possible to refer to the second half of the first millennium BC and the beginning of the first millennium AD as the High Iron Age.[1] Technological advances and interregional trade of the previous three millennia were now felt from the Alps to the Arctic Circle and from the Atlantic to the Urals, not just by elites but also by inhabitants of remote villages. The High Iron Age was a mysterious world of ordinary farmers, skilled craftsmen, bands of warriors and powerful ritual and political leaders.

The La Tène style

When lake levels around the Alps dropped in the 1850s revealing the pile dwelling sites discussed in Chapter One, an Iron Age ritual deposit containing an assortment of swords, scabbards, shields and ornaments was discovered at La Tène at the northern end of

Gold-plated bronze shield boss with La Tène decoration from Auvers-sur-Oise, France, in the Cabinet des Médailles of the Bibliothèque nationale in Paris.

Lake Neuchâtel. Their distinctive decoration led to the name of the site being adopted to refer to the decorative style of the final centuries BC in western Europe. The La Tène style is based on elegant curvilinear motifs, often evoking vines and leaves as well as geometric patterns and stylized human and animal forms. Over time, it became more abstract and fluid. Mainly executed on objects of bronze, silver and gold, variations of La Tène decoration provide cultural and chronological markers.

Scholars consider the La Tène style to be truly artistic in its technical sophistication, expressiveness and beauty. It was inspired by stylistic elements from Greek art, particularly its 'Orientalizing' phase, and Etruscan designs. These reached the Barbarian World along trade routes across the Alps during the second half of the first millennium BC. Craftsmen in temperate Europe took

Mediterranean models and expanded on them, like jazz musicians spontaneously improvising on a melody, allowing creativity and technical expertise to take them in new directions.

Regional La Tène styles soon developed. Perhaps the most extraordinary was the 'insular style' of the British Isles. On shields, the backs of mirrors and ornaments, craftsmen in Britain and Ireland took continental motifs and refined them into abstract tendrils and scrolls, highlighted with infilling. Although Roman conquest of Gaul and England caused the La Tène style to decline in those areas, it continued to flourish in Ireland and Scotland during the first centuries AD. Eventually, it was translated into the great illuminated manuscripts and other decorative arts. The exotic animals seen in the Book of Kells and 'Celtic' knots in traditional Irish decoration trace their roots to the La Tène style in the final centuries BC.

Fenced farmsteads

Across the Barbarian World, most people continued to live in small farmsteads. In southern Scandinavia, many settlements consisted of a cluster of farmsteads surrounded by a common fence.[2] The fences served a functional and a symbolic purpose. Functionally, they protected gardens from livestock during the growing season, and during the winter they contained the animals kept in one end of the houses. Symbolically, they reflected communal identity among the households that shared the enclosure. The farmsteads were not close together, so the fence meandered around them, occasionally interrupted by gates.

Houses in northern Europe were mainly 'three-aisled' long-houses, with two rows of interior posts and exterior walls made from wattle, daub and turf, 15–30 metres (50–100 ft) long. Around 200 BC, Grøntoft in Denmark contained nine longhouses and a barn. Later, during the first century AD, the nearby site of Hodde had up to 27 houses, with some situated just outside the fence. A similar trend towards settlement nucleation is seen in the Nether-lands. Bronze Age and early Iron Age settlements there have been characterized as dispersed and 'wandering',[3] meaning that

Reconstructed Iron Age roundhouse at Butser Ancient Farm, Hampshire.

farmsteads were not rebuilt on the same site but were abandoned and relocated some distance away. By the High Iron Age, however, farmsteads began to be clustered together and to be rebuilt, suggesting multigenerational occupation.[4]

In the British Isles, roundhouses continued as the norm, with a range of 5–15 metres (16–50 ft) in diameter. Wattle and daub walls (or stone in northern and western areas) were surmounted by conical pitched roofs. Each community was composed of several houses, with regional variations in the architectural details. As on the Continent, fences and enclosures demarcated farmsteads and structured community space. In the west of England, wetland settlements at Glastonbury and Meare have been studied for over a century.[5] At Glastonbury, over forty houses were found, with up to fourteen occupied at any one time before the settlement was abandoned about 50 BC.[6]

Although High Iron Age economy was a mix of farming and herding, domestic animals were especially important, not only for meat, milk and hides but also as the foundation of wealth and accumulation. Ownership of livestock became a pathway for social advancement during the final centuries BC. It enabled participation in the consumption economy connected with imports of Mediterranean products and eventually the introduction of coinage in western Europe.

Heterarchy

For many years, scholars assumed that ancient societies proceeded from an early stage of egalitarian social relations through increasingly hierarchical structures with more and more levels. In hierarchical systems, decisions at higher levels affect lower levels, and lines of authority run clearly to a paramount leader. Despite considerable evidence for social differentiation, however, it is difficult to fit High Iron Age societies into such a scheme of cultural evolution.

Instead, it seems possible that social arrangements in the Barbarian World corresponded more to a condition that could be called 'heterarchy',[7] in which there were varying pathways to status, power and influence. Relationships among households, clans, tribes and other social units were no less complex but were not tiered in the same way as a hierarchy. Practices of authority and deference were fluid and situational, perhaps more unstable over time.

A heterarchical system does not mean there were no leaders. The desire to achieve power through wealth and status is always motivation for individuals so inclined. It simply means that leaders may have been only one point of authority rather than an all-powerful apex, and individuals and communities had other sources of power and influence, which were adapted as times required. Sacrificial rituals needed priests (perhaps the Druids described by Caesar) to mediate between mortals and gods, while military adventures were led by individuals with distinction in fighting.

It is difficult to prove the existence of heterarchy, but it must be considered as an option given that evidence for paramount leaders who combined political, ritual and military functions is so slim. During the High Iron Age, characterizing social arrangements as heterarchy explains how the Romans who encountered barbarian groups were unable to fit them into their understanding of how civilized society should function. Barbarian society was complex but differed from the Roman social system in its ability to accommodate equivalences and differences in social standing and to distribute authority among multiple individuals.

Trackways

The bogs of northern Europe were obstacles to movement, not just for people, but especially for wagons and carts. Prehistoric people in wetland areas constructed wooden 'trackways' that became increasingly sophisticated over time.[8] They are preserved in waterlogged peat and found during cutting the peat for fuel or drainage. Important trackways from the last few centuries BC are found in northern Germany and adjacent areas of the Netherlands, lake basins in southern Germany such as the Federsee and in Ireland.

Running for over 2 kilometres (1¼ mi.) in Co. Longford, the Corlea trackway is one of the best studied in Ireland.[9] It is a road of oak planks about 4 metres (13 ft) long laid across parallel runners of oak and ash up to 10 metres (33 ft) long on the bog surface. Planks were pinned in place with stakes driven through holes in the ends. It required a coordinated effort to build, considering the need to fell oak trees, split them into planks, transport them to the work site and lay them next to each other. It is estimated that obtaining the 400 or so trees needed to make the 6,000 planks and associated runners and other parts required the clearance of 25 hectares (62 acres) of woodland. From tree-ring dating, we know the timbers were felled in 148 BC. Although the Corlea trackway is just over 1.6 kilometres (1 mi.) long, it was a crucial

Reconstructed Iron Age trackway in Corlea Bog, Co. Longford, Ireland.

connection in a major east–west route across the peatlands of central Ireland.

Building trackways may have been just as important as using them. Wooden vessels at Corlea suggest that work parties were fuelled by feasting and drinking. There was also a connection between the use of bogs for ritual activities. Spear shafts, mallets, yokes and pieces of unused wheels are found near trackways in Ireland, while carvings interpreted as human effigies were discovered at Corlea and at Wittemoor in Germany. Bogs are dynamic landscapes, and most trackways were rarely maintained for long. The Corlea trackway, for example, may have been used for ten years or less.

Water, sacrifice and human victims

Ceremonialism and the importance of watery places are running themes throughout the narrative of the Barbarian World. During the first millennium BC, sacrificial ceremonies took new turns. One was the interplay between warfare and sacrifice. The other, and more intriguing, was the ritualized killing of people and their deposition in bogs.

Some of the most memorable and evocative evidence for ceremony, sacrifice and violence during the High Iron Age comes from bog bodies, dozens of human corpses found in peat bogs of northern and western Europe.[10] Their skin, internal organs and hair have been preserved due to the unusual qualities of peat bogs, acidic wetlands where vegetation grows faster than it decays and undecayed plant matter accumulates, often reaching considerable thickness. Peat was widely used for fuel where it was abundant, although today its main use is in gardens. In Scandinavia and the British Isles, peat was once cut by hand, whereas today large machines shave away layers of compressed vegetation and load it onto conveyor belts.

Bodies can be preserved in peat almost indefinitely until discovered by peat-cutters or found in pieces on conveyor belts. Waterlogged peats are poor in oxygen and do not contain the microorganisms that promote decay. A body has to be submerged quickly, however, lest decay set in while it is still exposed to the air. The acidic water in bogs is also inhospitable to microorganisms. Finally, a chemical produced by sphagnum moss, sphagnan, not only retards decay but actively promotes preservation. Sphagnan depletes calcium in a body, giving bacteria less to feed on. It is also a tanning agent. This is why the skin of bog bodies often looks like dark brown leather, and the bones are deformed or even missing.

The first recorded bog bodies were found in the eighteenth century, but they were thought to be recent victims of drowning or exposure. Subsequently, archaeologists realized that these were prehistoric corpses. During the twentieth century, many came to light in the Netherlands, northern Germany and especially Denmark. The global Depression in the 1930s, the Second World War and hard times after the war meant that peat was a cheap and easily obtained fuel for heating and cooking. When a hand, foot or head was found, archaeologists were often notified.

A woman's body found in 1938 in a bog at Bjældskov near Silkeborg in Denmark was about 25 years old, with her hair braided and tied in a pigtail. Her body was wrapped in a sheepskin and a cowhide cloak. Yet Elling Woman, as she is known, did not die peacefully. A groove around her neck showed that she had been strangled, either by hanging or garrotting, perhaps with a leather rope found nearby. Thus began what might be called the Golden Age of Bog Bodies.

After the Second World War, peat cutting in Denmark and northern Germany continued intensively. In 1950, another body was found about 70 metres (230 ft) from Elling Woman. The block of peat containing it was cut out and taken back to the National Museum in Copenhagen to be excavated carefully. This bog was known locally as 'Tollund', and thus the superbly preserved corpse of a man 40–50 years old became 'Tollund Man'. Like Ötzi the Iceman, Tollund Man became a celebrity and even today is probably the best known of the bog bodies.[11]

Like Elling Woman, Tollund Man also died from strangulation. The braided leather rope was still around his neck. Except for a leather belt and conical leather cap, he was naked, curled up in a crouched position. Tollund Man's face is strangely serene, as if

Upper body of Windeby Boy on display at the Archäologisches Landesmuseum, Gottorf Castle, Schleswig, Germany; the textile band around the head is a modern replacement for the original.

he accepted his fate peacefully. After eating a final gruel of barley, wheat and flax, he probably walked down the valley path to his fate in the bog.

The year 1952 was a banner year for bog bodies, perhaps because peat-cutters were alive to the possibility that a corpse or body parts might appear, necessitating notification of archaeologists. Peat-cutters working near Windeby in northern Germany noticed human limbs on their conveyor belt and traced them to a spot in the bog. Investigation showed that there were actually two corpses. One was an elderly man whose bones had completely decalcified (perhaps because of his age) and his body pressed flat. The other

Torso of Huldremose Woman with her skin preserved but bones demineralized; we know that her final meal was rye bread.

was a remarkably well-preserved body of what was thought to be a teenage girl, naked except for a leather collar and a strip of cloth over her eyes. Her blond hair had been shaved on one side of her head. Apparently Windeby Girl met her death by drowning. A large stone and some branches had been used to hold her down. There is a recent twist, however. Closer examination revealed that Windeby Girl was probably Windeby Boy, a malnourished and sickly lad.[12]

That same year, peat-cutters at Grauballe, about 18 kilometres (11 mi.) from Tollund, found another body. This time, the block of peat was taken to the Moesgård Museum in Aarhus,[13] and Grauballe Man was carefully freed. He was lying on his chest, naked, with his left leg extended and his arm and right leg flexed. There was no mistaking the cause of his death around age thirty: his throat had been slashed from ear to ear. Grauballe Man's stomach contained 63 species of plants. His hands did not show evidence of hard work, so he was probably not a farmer. Nonetheless, he suffered from periods of nutritional stress and had a degenerative spinal condition.

After the 1950s, discoveries of bog bodies became less frequent, largely due to declining use of peat for fuel. Suburban sprawl and its gardens, however, revived peat cutting during the 1980s. In the British Isles, peat extraction is a big business. In 1984, a worker at a peat plant at Lindow Moss outside Manchester tossed a block of peat towards a co-worker. A human foot popped out when it hit the ground. Imagine that moment. More of the body was back at the cutting site. It was a man about 25 years old, 1.7 metres (5 ft 6 in.) tall, with a beard and moustache, naked except for a band of fox fur on one arm. His trimmed fingernails suggested a life without physical labour. Lindow Man died several violent deaths. He had been struck twice on the skull and garrotted. To make sure he was dead, his throat was slashed.[14]

The year 2003, like 1952, was a good one for bog bodies, this time in Ireland. Two bodies were found 40 kilometres (25 mi.) apart in the central Irish boglands, Clonycavan Man in Co. Meath and Oldcroghan Man in Co. Offaly, not far from the Corlea trackway.[15] Oldcroghan Man was very tall, standing about 2 metres (6 ft 6 in.)

in height. Like Grauballe Man and Lindow Man, his smooth and well-manicured hands suggested that he was not accustomed to manual labour. His fingernails indicated that he had eaten a meat-rich diet, although his last meal, as with many of the Danish victims, was a gruel of grains and milk. He died between 362 and 175 BC. Clonycavan Man, on the other hand, was very short, standing 1.57 metres (5 ft 2 in). Radiocarbon dating indicates that he died between 392 and 201 BC. His hair is spectacularly well preserved and styled with a gel of pine resin. This pomade came from pines that only grow in Spain and southwestern France, reflecting long-range connections along the Atlantic seaboard.

Consistent with the general theme, both Clonycavan Man and Oldcroghan Man met gruesome ends, but their killings were a little more imaginative than simple strangulation. Clonycavan Man was killed by three blows to the head, which split open his skull, and one more blow to the body from an axe before being disembowelled. Oldcroghan Man was bound with bands of hazel, which pierced his upper arms. He was then stabbed in the chest, decapitated and cut in half across his torso. Both men's nipples had been cut.

This last fact aroused the interest of archaeologists, since in ancient Ireland the practice of sucking a king's nipples was a gesture of submission. Ned Kelly of the National Museum of Ireland believes these men were either failed kings or failed prospective kings, and mutilation of their nipples meant that they were rendered incapable of kingship.[16] Whether or not this theory explains the gruesome deaths of these and several other Irish bog bodies, it seems likely that they were representatives of a social elite rather than common farmers and herders.

We do not know the motivation for these sacrifices. Analogies to animistic societies are simply speculations. We have some idea of Celtic deities, but which, if any, demanded such sacrifice? Were the victims willing or under duress? At the moment, we have to look somewhat dispassionately at these grisly practices and treat them as a fact of Iron Age life, as well as a tremendous source of information, in the same way Ötzi the Iceman continues to provide revelations about his life and death.

Like Ötzi, bog bodies provide a human face, albeit a very atypical one, of Iron Age people in northern Europe. When they invaded Gaul, Britain and Germany, the Romans met peoples with the ideology and values that led them to conduct such sacrificial killings and to consider wetlands and bogs to be places for sacred ceremonies. Although they seem gruesome, the killings were routine practices. Ordinary Iron Age people may have been desensitized to them or regarded them as the price of belonging to the social elite. They are emblematic, however, of a world in which deities and sacrifice were connected with specific landscape features. Such sacralized landscapes must have existed for millennia, but during the High Iron Age they reached the pinnacle of their significance with the addition of humans to the deposition, even if we do not know to what Moloch they were sacrificed.

Water, sacrifice and war booty

Adding credence to the belief that bog bodies were sacrificial victims is the fact that war booty also began to play a role in votive offerings during the Iron Age in southern Scandinavia around the same time. In addition to the sacral nature of wetlands, another barbarian theme, movement across water, comes forth yet again. An early example of this practice is the Hjortspring Boat on the Danish island of Als.

In the small Hjortspring bog, nineteenth-century peat-diggers discovered and damaged a large wooden boat, which was not excavated until the 1920s. Besides boat fragments, archaeologists found several hundred weapons, animal bones and wooden artefacts. Additional excavations in 1987 turned up further pieces of the boat. Radiocarbon dates on the newly found pieces indicated that the Hjortspring Boat dates to 350–300 BC, earlier than expected.[17]

Stem to stern the boat was 19 metres (62 ft) long, with a bottom plank and two long strakes on each side, extended to form upturned prows. Planks of linden wood make up the hull. The interior was 13 metres (43 ft) long and just under 2 metres (6 ft) wide, with ten crossbeams forming seats. Assuming twenty rowers on the crossbeams, one or two helmsmen and perhaps a lookout, the crew of the Hjortspring Boat probably numbered 22–24 people. They could have carried it easily, and the flat bottom made it possible to arrive on sandy beaches and glide over sandbars. Its overall form echoes the schematic Bronze Age rock carvings from several centuries earlier.

The Hjortspring Boat was not simply abandoned. The objects mark it as a major sacrificial weapon find, the earliest from Denmark. Most were spearheads, 138 of iron and 31 of bone or antler. Some still had broken-off pieces of ash-wood shafts in their sockets. The Hjortspring deposit also contained eleven swords, two of which were deliberately bent. Wooden shields, nearly eighty in all, were oval or rectangular in varying widths, each with a handle at the centre. At one end of the boat, rust prints of many small iron rings represented traces of chain mail, the earliest in Europe. Based on their area, it is estimated that ten to twenty sets of chain mail were deposited with the boat.

The Hjortspring Boat is interpreted as an offering made by victors. It is possible that the boat and weapons were the equipment of a foe, with the assumption that the defeated party arrived in the boat. Klavs Randsborg calculates the number of shields and spears to indicate a force of about eighty fighters.[18] If a Hjortspring-type boat could accommodate 20–24 warriors, then the weapons represent the equipment of four boatloads. Violence was a constant threat in the Barbarian World, but now it was necessary to contend with organized raiding parties of heavily armed warriors coming out of the mist, beaching their boats and attacking farmsteads and villages. It seems, however, that the inhabitants of Als were also competent fighters, for these marauders evidently met an unhappy end. It was deemed more important to sacrifice the weapons and equipment rather than retain them for future use, an indication of powerful spiritual forces that governed the lives of people during the High Iron Age.

The *oppida*

During the last three centuries BC, another wave of settlement agglomeration swept across the Barbarian World. These large sites

Reconstruction of the Hjortspring Boat at the National Museum in Copenhagen.

are called *oppida* (singular *oppidum*), a term used by Julius Caesar in *De Bello Gallico* for fortified centres of native settlement. *Oppida* are usually located on hilltops, plateaus or other strategic landmarks, although some, like Manching in Bavaria, are on flat ground. Many were built on places already used for ritual gatherings or large open settlements, while others were built on new locations. In some cases, unfortified settlements were abandoned and their inhabitants moved into a new *oppidum* nearby.

From the outside, the *oppida* were recognized by their fortifications. In western Europe, and as far east as Manching, the ramparts of *oppida* were built using a technique Caesar called *murus Gallicus*. Outer stone walls 3–6 m (10–20 ft) apart were tied together with heavy timbers spaced horizontally and vertically. Between the walls, longer timbers running lengthwise with the wall were pinned to the cross-timbers with iron spikes. Finally, the

Wooden shield from Hjortspring.

space between the walls and around the timbers was filled with stones and earth. The result was a strong and fireproof rampart, often backed on the inside of the *oppidum* by an earthen ramp so defenders could reach the top. Gates permitted access to the interior, often leading directly onto main arterial streets.

In addition to a residential function, *oppida* served as centres for the production of luxury goods and as nodes in trading networks that brought products of Italian workshops and vineyards to temperate Europe. Internal differentiation into neighbourhoods of elites, commoners and industrial zones gave them what some consider an urban character. Large palisaded enclosures were elite farmsteads with large houses and outbuildings, while craftsmen and farmers lived and worked in smaller buildings. Streets defined corridors of movement and gave the *oppida* internal organization. *Oppida* also had administrative functions as the centres of tribal polities. Tribute and tolls were collected, mints produced coins and they were seats of governmental and legal bodies.

Archaeologists debate the urban character of *oppida*. In their combination of residential, market, industrial, administrative and ritual functions, they are clearly different from hillforts. At the same time, their low-density occupations differ from the modern idea of a proper city. Urbanists speak of 'compact' and 'dispersed' cities, and *oppida* seem to approach the latter category. Perhaps 'fortified towns' is the best characterization for now, reserving the word 'city' for larger, higher-density and more persistent forms. Had Caesar not invaded Gaul, many *oppida* might have become nuclei of cities across western Europe rather than lonely abandoned ramparts.

Bibracte

Located strategically on the portage between the Saône river (which leads south to the Rhône and the Mediterranean) and the Yonne (draining to the Seine and the English Channel), Bibracte is a classic Gallic *oppidum*. Today, it is known as Mont Beuvray, a hilltop ringed by two *murus Gallicus* ramparts. The exterior rampart encloses about 200 hectares (500 acres), while the inner one encircles about 135 hectares (333 acres). The length of these fortifications made them indefensible to attacks at multiple points, so they were mainly for show.

Bibracte was founded in the late second century BC and flourished for most of the first century BC. Specialist manufacturing districts for bronze- and iron-working were situated along the main arterial road. Beyond lay residential precincts. Bibracte was a centre for consumption as well. Fragments of thousands of Italian wine amphorae have been found, and in one spot a road was paved with amphorae shards. Such evidence for wine consumption further documents intensive trade between Rome and Gaul even before the Roman conquest.

Caesar's campaigns and their aftermath brought Bibracte out of prehistory and into history. Here, Vercingetorix assembled a coalition of tribes and proclaimed their revolt against Rome in 52 BC. After defeating Vercingetorix at Alésia that September, Caesar repaired to Bibracte and spent the winter of 52–51 BC writing his account of the Gallic Wars. He observed the functioning of native society, including its election of a chief magistrate, formation of an assembly and sources of income, such as tolls on traders.

After the middle of the first century BC, there was considerable development of public and private buildings at Bibracte, including Mediterranean-style houses with courtyards and a basilica in the Roman style. A cremation cemetery was located outside the ramparts. Despite this investment, Bibracte declined at the end of the first century BC. Its population moved to Augustodunum, the modern city of Autun, 27 kilometres (17 mi.) away.

Romans meet the Barbarians

From the first century BC onward, it is impossible to discuss the Barbarian World without including the Romans. Not only did Roman armies conquer much of western Europe, but the Roman presence was felt far beyond the Imperial frontiers. The Roman conquest of Gaul and southern Britain transformed the native societies of these areas and caused the Barbarian World to shrink. Barbarians living under Roman rule became part of the Roman World.

The barbarians of Gaul and Britain were already familiar with Romans. A lively trade in luxury Roman goods and wine prospered throughout this region during the final centuries BC, as is evident at Bibracte and other *oppida*. After the Romans conquered northern Italy during the third century BC, and took control of modern Provence (its name derived from having been a Roman province) in the second century BC, they were not only on the doorstep but already in the foyer of the Barbarian World. Caesar's forays north starting in 58 BC established Roman military occupation and administrative control in areas already permeated with Roman objects and cultural practices.

Contact and 'Romanization'

The impact of Roman conquest on the barbarians of western Europe has been debated by scholars. Romans were able to integrate many different peoples into a complex cultural mosaic. From the Roman perspective, as articulated through classical accounts, they exerted a firm civilizing influence over the barbarian natives, who recognized the superiority of Roman artefacts and practices.

Another point of view is more anthropological and fits with an interpretation of the archaeological record, in which native elites adopted Roman practices such as living in Roman-style towns and speaking Latin in order to enhance their own positions. Both of these perspectives, however, simplify a very complex blending of Roman and barbarian societies during the final century BC and first centuries AD.

A simple Roman/native binary division did not exist, except on the battlefield during the first years of Roman conquest. Roman military power was real (although not invincible), and with it came Roman cultural domination. Neither was as suffocating as one might infer from traditional accounts. New trends and fashions, along with shifting political and military alignments, evolved in the Roman heartland in Italy and were adopted by Romans and natives in the provinces. Over time, this cultural transfer became

Bibracte (modern Mont Beuvray), reconstruction of gate showing *murus Gallicus* wall construction.

a two-way street, with barbarian products and customs and even barbarians themselves incorporated into Roman society. Thus the concept of 'Romanization' of native peoples has been largely abandoned in favour of recognition that the interrelationship was much more complicated.

In territorial conquests familiar from recent centuries, the conquering power decapitates a native hierarchy and imposes its own authority at all levels. The Romans in western Europe could not do this, I suggest, due to the heterarchical structure of High Iron Age society. With multiple lines of authority and leadership in the Barbarian World, all Romans could do was keep the native elites in place and work with them, exerting power through military occupation and parallel Roman officials. This patron–client arrangement worked adequately, so long as natives deferred to Roman Imperial authority and paid their taxes, while continuing to manage their affairs as they had done before the Romans arrived. Client dynasties persisted from one generation to the next, and conflicts and intrigues kept them in check. If necessary, the Romans could pick a winner at the point of a spear.

Romans in Gaul and Britain

Until the middle of the first century BC, the only contacts the Barbarian World had with Mediterranean civilizations were largely in the commercial sphere, or through movement of barbarians southward into areas loosely incorporated into the world of classical urban states. The entrance of Roman armies under Julius Caesar into Gaul north and west of the Alps marked a change in the relationship between barbarians and Mediterranean civilization. No longer did Romans just want to obtain slaves and hides in exchange for wine and luxury goods. They wanted barbarian land.

The story of Caesar's conquest of Gaul, his forays to Britain and his troubles with natives is well known from not only his own accounts but also the works of other classical authors. These narratives are generally supported by archaeology, which fills in gaps about the societies that Caesar encountered. *Oppida* play a central role in this story. Roman rule did not transform barbarian societies overnight, but during the next several decades the natives of Gaul adopted Roman ways of life and thus moved from prehistory onto the pages of history.

Although Caesar portrayed his expeditions to Britain in 55 and 54 BC as forays into an unknown world, this was really propaganda designed to make him look daring. Romans had known about Britain for a long time, while the people of Britain had been aware of events to their south, as well as the fact that they could obtain desirable products from Gaul that came from the Mediterranean world.

The rivers Avon and Stour converge on the coast of southern England near a sandstone promontory called Hengistbury Head.[19] Hengistbury Head shelters a fine harbour and was a prominent feature spotted easily by a navigator sailing north from Brittany. By the end of the first millennium BC, it had been an established landmark for millennia, since settlement from the Stone Age and Bronze Age is found there.

Around 100 BC, Hengistbury Head's harbour emerged as a major port-of-trade for goods entering southern Britain from Continental Europe. Coins and pottery found there can be traced to specific sites in the ancient region of Armorica (northern Brittany). Goods that passed through Hengistbury included amphorae of Italian wine, metal objects, glass and figs. These products were exchanged for British products that included grain, silver, gold, copper, iron and probably hides. Iron-bearing rock was mined and smelted at Hengistbury Head itself. Finds at Hengistbury Head show that thriving commercial connections between Continental Europe and the British Isles already existed prior to Caesar's conquest of Gaul, with products of Mediterranean vineyards and workshops in demand across the English Channel.

Caesar's brief incursions into southern England in 55 and 54 BC disrupted the trade network through Hengistbury. The reasons for this are not entirely clear. Instead, the main axis of contact between Continental Europe and Britain shifted east during the second half of the first century BC, from northeastern France and Belgium to Kent and the Thames Estuary.[20] Roman merchants set up shop in southeast England, doing business in olive and fish oil, wine, tableware, glass bowls and high-quality metal goods. Along with objects, Gallo-Belgic practices arrived in Britain, including the style of cremation burial used on the European mainland.

For the moment, Britain remained part of the Barbarian World outside Roman military and administrative control. During the late first century BC and the early first century AD, the Romans cultivated barbarian elites in southern England who ruled small tribal states, turning them into client dynasties. Barbarian leaders in political hot water occasionally fled across the Channel to seek Roman protection. Gradually, between 54 BC and AD 43, southern Britain was pulled into the Roman World.

Romans finally arrived as a military force in Britain in the summer of AD 43. Four legions with auxiliary troops probably landed at several points in Kent. By the winter of 43, Romans had secured a foothold in Kent and along the lower Thames by taking control of tribal capitals that later became the Roman towns of Camulodunum (Colchester) and Verulamium (St Albans). Over the following years, Roman forces moved west and north to seize native strongholds like Maiden Castle. Imposing their authority on friendly client kings was straightforward, but elsewhere they met resistance, especially in the west. By AD 49, Roman troops were overseeing mining of silver and lead from the Mendip Hills near the Bristol Channel, and their control of the seas gave them access to harbours along the south coast.

The Roman frontiers in Germania

The Romans had their own name for the Barbarian World that lay along the Rhine river and beyond: Germania. Areas on the west bank of the Rhine were incorporated into the Roman Empire by Caesar as part of his conquest of Gaul and became known as Lesser Germania, divided into two provinces. Lower Germania (Germania Inferior) corresponded to the Benelux countries and the Rhineland, while Upper Germania (Germania Superior) covered modern Alsace and northwestern Switzerland. Beyond the Rhine lay Greater Germania (Germania Magna), stretching indefinitely to the east. While the border between Lesser and Greater

Cross-section of Roman wine amphora of the Dressel 1B type, one of the most common found in Gaul and Britain during the first millennium BC.

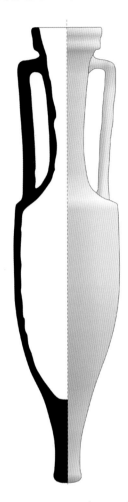

Germania was permeable, Caesar never went beyond the Rhine during his conquests. Instead, relationships were developed with client kings and dynasties similar to those with the elites in Britain. Barbarian warlords in Germania Magna became cosy with Roman authorities across the Rhine, and their subjects not only traded with Roman-occupied zones but also picked up Roman cultural practices. Some served in the Roman army, starting a tradition that culminated several centuries later.

Client kings and warlords

In Gaul and Lesser Germania, Roman authorities did not replace the native elites but rather were layered on top of them. They could enforce their wishes through military force, so native leaders did not dare cross them. The Romans also took advantage of highly elastic tribal affiliations among the barbarians to manipulate and restructure their ethnic identities.

As an example of such top-down restructuring, Dutch archaeologist Nico Roymans describes three aspects of Roman Imperial policy towards conquered peoples in frontier zones, with specific reference to Germania Inferior between about 50 BC and AD 70.[21] In this area, the Romans ruthlessly destroyed tribes such as the Eburones and Aduatuci who resisted or revolted, created new tribal polities such as the Batavians and Ubii by resettling groups who crossed the Rhine from Germania Magna, and fostered new tribal identities as ethnic soldiers. An analogy can be made between Batavians as troop suppliers to the Roman Empire and Nepalese Gurkhas as ethnic fighting units in the British Army.

Roman rule also provided social mobility strategies for barbarian elites in the occupied territories and adjacent regions. Some hitched their wagons to the Romans, welcoming their new overlords and being good clients, making money through trade and soldiering. Others saw anti-Romanism as a way to advance, by fomenting revolt and conspiracies against the occupiers, obviously a much riskier strategy. Some natives tried to do both, as we will see below in the case of Arminius. Roman Imperial policy in the frontier zone during the final decades BC and through the first century AD was an unstable mix of colonization, repression, collaboration with local dynasties and fear of rebellion. Underneath Roman authority was competition among barbarian elites for leadership and prestige in their own polities.

Things end badly beyond the Rhine

During the final decades BC and the first decades AD, Roman forces made several forays beyond the Rhine. Knowledge of these activities has come down to us through the classical writers and recently through archaeology, but it is likely that more such adventures were not documented. Although eventual conquest may have been a strategic goal, these expeditions were not designed to occupy territory. Instead, their near-term goal was to demonstrate Roman power and intimidate the barbarian tribes into submission. They also had the goal of establishing working relationships with tractable elites in barbarian polities.

These expeditions resemble the Spanish marches through what is now the southeastern United States during the sixteenth century, in which heavily armed groups of professional soldiers made deep penetrations into territory controlled by Mississippian tribes. The most famous is the de Soto Expedition, or *entrada*, which started from Florida and took a route through most of the southern states, crossed the Mississippi and was eventually evacuated from the Texas coast. The de Soto *entrada* left few physical traces, but its route has been reconstructed from contemporary accounts and connections with archaeological sites. It seems similar to Roman *entradas* in Germania Magna 1,500 years earlier, although the latter were over shorter distances and across terrain that became increasingly familiar to the Romans.

The first expeditions into Germania Magna were undertaken by Drusus, a stepson of Augustus. In 11 BC, he crossed the Rhine and marched to the Weser, a river that drains into the North Sea near the modern city of Bremen. One of his camps has been found at Oberaden, where timbers dated by tree rings were felled in the late summer or autumn of 11 BC.[22] Drusus' *entrada* aroused the hostility of native tribes so he had to carry out a fighting retreat to the Rhine. Two years later, Drusus marched all the way to the Elbe, the next great northward-draining river beyond the Rhine. This expedition was conducted more assertively, but upon reaching the Elbe, Drusus turned around and marched back to the Rhine. On the return route, he fell from his horse and died from his injuries. Other than providing propaganda for consumption back in Rome, Drusus' *entradas* did little to expand Rome's authority.

In AD 5, Tiberius, the other stepson of Augustus, came north from Pannonia and led a fighting expedition to the lower Elbe,

Reconstructed statue of Augustus at Waldgirmes, Lahnau, Germany.

where he met Roman ships coming in from the North Sea. Tiberius set up several advanced bases east of the Rhine. The most important one was at Haltern on the Lippe river, 18 kilometres (11 mi.) from where it flows into the Rhine. The Lippe is one of the few west–east river corridors in this part of Europe, and the Romans regarded it as a prime route into Germania Magna. Haltern quickly developed into a complex of fortified camps and a naval harbour.

As the United States found out in Vietnam, fortified camps do not exert control over the surrounding area. Nonetheless, Augustus seems to have believed that the Rhine–Elbe zone was under Roman control and shifted his attention elsewhere. An open question, however, is whether he intended to turn this area into a proper Roman province with an administrative structure to carry out activities such as taking a census and collecting taxes.

A Roman complex at Waldgirmes seems to point in this direction.[23] Waldgirmes is about 100 kilometres (60 mi.) from the Rhine, deep in Germania Magna. The site covers 7.7 hectares (19 acres) and is surrounded by ditches backed by a timber palisade. Yet Waldgirmes was not a military camp, for it lacks the typical layout of a Roman fort. Instead, its buildings have a non-military character, including a forum and a basilica, and houses and pottery kilns mark it as a Roman civilian community. In addition to civic and domestic buildings, the Romans also installed visual trappings of Augustan authority. A gilded bronze equestrian statue depicted Augustus in his glory.

The problem was that the surrounding territory was not dominated by Romans. Instead, the area between the Rhine and the Elbe at the start of the first millennium AD was a patchwork of small polities, chiefs and kings with varying degrees of affection for Rome, warlords and fluid allegiances. In other words, it was a typical High Iron Age heterarchy, which the Romans had difficulty figuring out. Since they seemed reluctant to conquer Germania Magna by overwhelming force as they had done in Gaul, the area remained a complicated borderland, both desirable and mysterious.

Publius Quinctilius Varus, a long-time Roman provincial administrator linked to Augustus by marriage, became governor of the Rhineland in AD 7. Two years later, he led three legions, about 20,000 men, plus auxiliary troops on an expedition across the Rhine. Returning, Varus learned of a rebellion against a Roman client and decided to suppress it. To get there, he took an unfamiliar route along the northern edge of hills known today as the Teutoberg Forest north of the modern city of Osnabrück.

According to written sources, which the reader always must remember were composed decades or centuries later, Varus learned about the rebellion from a Roman client named Arminius. Arminius is an interesting character who steps out of the Barbarian World into history. He was a member of the social elite in the Cherusci who lived along the lower Weser. The Cherusci seem to have had a love–hate relationship with the Romans, at times being allies or clients and at others being mortal enemies. Arminius came out of this ambivalent relationship to serve in a Roman auxiliary unit in Pannonia. Back in Germania Magna, however, he loathed the Romans and quietly mobilized an alliance of tribes against them.

The route taken by Varus led through unfamiliar terrain covered with forests and bogs. His legionaries entered a narrow defile between a hill known as the Kalkriese on the south and a large bog on the north. This was a bad idea. Roman equipment and tactics were developed for dryland areas with room for manoeuvre. Legionaries were not accustomed to fighting among wetlands. Moreover, Arminius and his tribesmen had literally shaped the battlefield by building a large sod wall along the bottom of the hill. When Varus and his legions tried to thread this narrow valley, Arminius sprang his trap.

There are no eyewitness accounts of the slaughter that followed, but Varus' legions were wiped out. Even the site of the battle was unknown until 1987. Here is where archaeology takes over from fragmentary and conflicting third-hand accounts.

In 1987, Tony Clunn (1946–2014) was an officer with the British Army of the Rhine.[24] He was also a metal detector enthusiast. In Osnabrück, he contacted local archaeologists about promising places to conduct his hobby. Surprisingly, given how archaeologists then viewed metal-detectorists, they directed him towards an area near the Kalkriese where Roman coins had previously been

The slaughter at the Kalkriese: *Varusschlacht* by Otto Albert Koch, 1909.

found. Clunn soon came across three Roman lead slingstones, which would have been used by legionaries who specialized in the use of the sling. He informed his archaeologist colleagues, who commenced excavations that resulted in an immense find of Roman weaponry, numbering in the thousands, along with bones of adult men and mules. Among the finds were Roman spear points; *ballista* bolts; bronze, gold and silver trim from weapons

Cache of silver denarii discovered in 1987 at the site of the ambush of the Roman legions in the Teutoberg Forest.

and belts; thousands of hobnails from boots; and many coins no later than AD 9. The likely site of Arminius' ambush had been found.

The finds from the area between the Kalkriese and the bog permit the reconstruction of the slaughter and its aftermath. American archaeologist Peter Wells has woven the sources together into a compelling narrative, which is well worth reading.[25] In particular, the foot of the turf wall was the scene of exceptional violence. Roman tactics and body armour were no match for heavy barbarian spears hurled from above.

The weapons and the bodies of the dead Romans were left in place after the battle. Why would the victorious tribesmen have done this? Here, war-booty offerings like the Hjortspring Boat provide an explanation. It seems that the site was treated as a weapons sacrifice, a giant ritual deposit. The bog at the Kalkriese had previously been used for offerings, so its proximity to the ambush made it a natural candidate for such a sacrifice. Rotting Roman corpses and eventually skeletons must have formed a macabre tableau that held powerful significance for the victorious Cherusci and their allies.[26]

The defeat of Varus effectively ended Roman plans to turn the land beyond the Rhine into a province. Terror swept the Roman camps and towns established in this area. Again, archaeology provides details. The base at Haltern was abandoned quickly as fear of Arminius swept the Lippe valley. Whole *terra sigillata* (fine pottery made in workshops in Italy and Gaul) vessels were left in place. The skeletons of 24 individuals in a Haltern kiln are a mystery.[27] Were they Romans or Germans, civilians or soldiers? If Germans, were they on the Roman or the barbarian side?

It had been thought that Waldgirmes was abandoned about the same time. Recently, however, evidence has emerged that it may have been active a bit longer.[28] A well yielded waterlogged wooden objects, including containers, building elements and pieces of ladders. Tree rings indicate that the ladders were made in the autumn or winter of AD 9, shortly after Varus' defeat. Assuming they remained in use for a while, it seems that Waldgirmes persisted a few more years. By the middle of the next decade, however, Waldgirmes was certainly empty of Romans and deserted.

The defeat of Varus marked the end of Roman Imperial expansion beyond the Rhine. Loss of three legions (their numbers were never reused) caused anguish in Rome. It also permanently changed the course of history by leaving the Barbarian World beyond the Rhine to the Baltic Sea and Scandinavia to develop in its own distinctive way. Archaeologically, Roman *entradas* into the Rhine–Elbe borderland provide glimpses into barbarian practices and customs that complement findings from discoveries elsewhere in northern Europe, as well as filling in details unavailable from written narratives.

Roman impact beyond the continental frontier

Despite Roman setbacks in Germania Magna, interaction and contact along the Rhine and the Danube continued. In the frontier zone, commerce flourished as local warlords and elites sought Roman goods. During the first century AD, Roman impact was felt even further into the Barbarian World. People living as far away as Poland and southern Scandinavia were aware that something big was happening to the west and southwest. Again, we must keep in mind the connectedness of the Barbarian World. People communicated with each other, and boundaries between small-scale polities were highly permeable, enabling travel by entrepreneurial people.

Of particular note are finds of Roman legionary equipment far beyond the Imperial frontier. At Siemiechów in central Poland, a Roman helmet was found in a cremation burial from the first century AD.[29] It was accompanied by a long sword that had been bent in three and other artefacts that point towards an origin in southern Germany. Was this individual an actual Roman legionary wandering deep in the Barbarian World? Or did the helmet, sword and other items arrive via trade or war booty from a barbarian raid on Roman legions along the Danube? Or were they sold, illegally, to barbarians and traded north along well-established routes?

Michael Meyer distinguishes between Roman goods entering the Barbarian World and 'intangible imports' that penetrated the frontier.[30] Roman objects that crossed the early Imperial frontier functioned either as status symbols or as raw materials. In Meyer's view, there is little evidence for 'constant and directed' long-distance trade with the Barbarian World. Once they found their way across the frontier, certain objects were highly valued for their Roman origin and authenticity, and in some cases, their superior characteristics. The quality of the Roman swords could not be matched by barbarian metalsmiths. Use of Roman objects did not signal a wish to 'become Roman' but rather they served as status markers within barbarian society.

Of equal significance, in Meyer's view, are what he calls 'intangible imports' adopted by barbarians. These include ceramic and metal technologies, styles of dress, table customs, perhaps religious practices and aspects of the organization of production and trade. For example, iron-working centres were established separately from settlements, such as the Holy Cross Mountains in central Poland.

Yet certain aspects of life in the Barbarian World remained untouched by Roman influence. Settlement structure in Germania Magna and beyond continued unchanged, and there was no adoption of Roman architecture. Crops and livestock also show no Roman influence. There was no trend towards breeding larger Roman-type cattle, for example.

The Gundestrup Cauldron: an icon of the High Iron Age

In 1891, peat-diggers in northern Jutland came upon a collection of curved silver plates. They fitted together to form the base, sides and rim of a large silver bowl, which has become familiar to archaeologists as the Gundestrup Cauldron.[31] The word 'cauldron' is more evocative than 'bowl', but the Gundestrup Cauldron was not meant for cooking over a fire but rather to be displayed, admired and read by all who saw it. It depicts a complicated spiritual world inhabited by gods, goddesses and exotic animals.

Made between 150 BC and AD 1, the Gundestrup Cauldron represents a convergence of major themes for understanding the Barbarian World. Almost certainly it came to Denmark from the Balkans. In technique and style, it is akin to objects found in Thracian kingdoms in Romania and Bulgaria. It is not the only imported bowl known from Iron Age Scandinavia. Others, such as a decorated bowl from Mosbæk, are of Etruscan, Greek or western European origin. Thus, the routes by which so many bronze objects ended up in Denmark over the previous two millennia had reached a point where a silverworker in the Balkans could produce an object whose iconography appealed to a Scandinavian.

The Gundestrup Cauldron is composed of a base, seven outer plates, five inner plates and a rim. Raised human and animal figures were embossed from behind. The outer plates show exotic figures interpreted as gods and goddesses along with animals, while the inner plates portray activities such as processions of warriors and bull sacrifices. Considerable planning went into the arrangement of the motifs and figures. Disassembly and inspection of the plates in 2002 revealed additional inscribed images, including a horn blower and a leonine figure, perhaps intended as patterns for embossing never carried out.

The Gundestrup Cauldron embodies many prominent features of the High Iron Age: long-distance acquisition, elite prestige,

The Gundestrup Cauldron, showing its composition of panels depicting deities and exotic animals. One of the most famous panels is in the interior right, showing an individual with an antler headdress holding a snake.

outstanding craftsmanship and complex spirituality. All had been prevalent in the Barbarian World for centuries, but here they reach a pinnacle in a single artefact. It travelled nearly 2,400 kilometres (1,500 mi.) to reach its destination, across lands populated by diverse communities and along dangerous roads and rivers. With it came knowledge of distant lands, transmitted from mouth to mouth and transmuted as information passed through filters in retelling. The deities it depicts inhabit an exotic universe, alien to everyday experience, populated by beings who consorted with lions, elephants and snakes. When displayed, before it was sacrificed in the bog, it must have been an object of awe and veneration. Whoever owned it was the master of his realm.

The Barbarian World in AD 100

By AD 100, the Barbarian World had shrunk considerably due to the absorption of Gaul, Lesser Germania and much of Britain into the Roman Empire. Only Ireland, Scotland, Scandinavia and the lands east of the Rhine and north of the Danube were still in the hands of barbarians. Even in these areas, the Roman Empire had an impact, and its products and practices passed through the porous frontier to be incorporated into the ways of Iron Age elites. Within the Empire, native peoples, barbarians by genome, continued many of their traditional ways and occasionally took up arms against their occupiers.

The heterarchy of the Barbarian World in which authority was distributed across many categories of society was most pronounced at this time. This social structure was the key organizational difference between the Barbarian World and the hierarchical Roman Empire with its delineated structure of deference and command. Barbarian kings shared power with priests and warriors who were successful in trade, battle, agriculture and ritual.

It was a violent time. A war party could descend without warning, gliding across water in increasingly sophisticated watercraft, and then celebrate their victory with a massive sacrifice of war booty. Ritual killings whose victims are found in bogs were common occurrences. Barbarians served as mercenaries in the

Roman army and learned its military practices, which could be turned against the Romans. Perhaps the reason the Romans made no further attempts to pacify Germania Magna was that native people had learned how to fight them.

Despite Roman occupation of much of it, the Barbarian World was as interconnected as ever. Britain and Continental Europe were bound together by trade and shared practices. Germania Magna and southern Scandinavia were also tightly coupled. Artefacts such as the Gundestrup Cauldron show how objects could be crafted far away from where they entered the archaeological record. The Roman Empire was starting to unravel, however, and the next several centuries were times of upheaval and change.

FIVE

BARBARIANS BEYOND THE IMPERIAL FRONTIER

B y the early second century AD, the Roman Imperial frontier had been more or less established in final form. In the north, Hadrian's Wall would soon be built across northern Britain between the North Sea and the Irish Sea to be a visible symbol of Roman power and to integrate garrisons along its length. The northern frontier in Britain would be further extended in AD 138 with the building of the Antonine Wall across the neck of Scotland, although Imperial control in the intervening area was short-lived. Ireland continued to lie outside the Roman frontier. Although some Roman artefacts are found in Ireland, no conclusive evidence of Roman settlement has appeared. This is not to say that no Roman ever set foot in Ireland. The island was clearly known to the Roman world, and commerce across the Irish Sea followed kinship connections that spanned Ireland, Scotland and Wales. Ptolemy's narrative and map, drawn from Roman military sources in the second century AD, shows Ireland and mentions specific tribes, such as the Iverni in today's Co. Cork.[1] According to Tacitus, around AD 81 the Roman general Agricola planned to invade Ireland and even had an Irish quisling ready to install as a leader, but disturbances in Scotland led to postponement of the invasion.

The Roman Imperial frontier in Continental Europe continued to be defined largely by the Rhine and Danube that formed the western and southern edges of Germania Magna.[2] It followed the Rhine past Cologne (Roman, Colonia Agrippina) to near Mainz (Roman, Mogontiacum). From there, it ran overland on lines that resulted from small Roman advances into the southern edge of

Germania Magna during the first and second centuries AD (the so-called Raetian Limes, or frontier) before reaching the Danube just upstream of the old *oppidum* at Kelheim. From there, the frontier continued downstream past Vienna (Roman, Vindobona) and around the Danube bend to Budapest (Roman, Aquincum). The land frontier across southern Germany was vulnerable, and thus it was heavily fortified with garrisons and watchtowers built in multiple layers along valleys and roads. Despite these fixed defences, the Raetian Limes were porous, and during the late third century AD they were largely abandoned in favour of a frontier along the upper Rhine and upper Danube.

Frontier hinterlands

The frontier during the late years of the Empire had a hinterland on both sides, so it was both a boundary and a borderland that extended for some distance into Roman-controlled territory on one side and a similar distance into barbarian lands on the other. On the Roman side, the frontier was also a fortified zone with a mix of legionary camps, civilian towns, villas and farms as well as native villages and farmsteads. Natives and Romans coexisted tensely but for the most part amicably. The population in the Roman provinces was a heterogeneous mix of people who had lived there previously, those who had been relocated from another part of the Empire and many who had moved into the Imperial zone from beyond the frontier. Roman administrative policy did not prevent this movement so long as it did not threaten the Empire's authority. Over time, natives began to assume positions within the Roman administrative structure.

On the other side of the frontier lay the barbarian lands. Those close to the frontier felt the Roman presence very strongly. There was a high intensity of interaction between people living in the Roman-controlled zone and those living just beyond it. Roman goods along with Romans themselves, passed through the permeable frontier fairly easily. The archaeologist Peter Wells describes a process of 'incorporation' in which non-state societies that interact with imperial states become interlinked economically and socially with the more powerful polity.³ Elites adopted Roman things to display their status and prestige, and barbarians crossed the frontier to serve in the Roman army. Despite tensions and sometimes open conflict, the 'default setting' for Roman–barbarian relations, according to the historian Guy Halsall, was 'quiet coexistence'.⁴

Areas close to the frontier were inundated with Roman goods, which then spread far and wide into the Barbarian World. By the third century AD, Roman-trained craftsmen were active in frontier areas on the barbarian side of the Rhine and Danube, making pottery and glass. Roman products reached the Barbarian World in several different ways. Trade across the frontier led to trading posts and emporia on the barbarian side of the frontier to facilitate commerce. Booty from military raids was a source of weapons. Roman subsidies and gifts to their clients, their pay to barbarian mercenaries and souvenirs brought back by mercenaries were also important conduits for Roman goods and coins. The gifts and subsidies to barbarian clients turned into tribute and payoffs to buy off hostile warlords and maintain peace and quiet. The Romans hoped that if they fed the barbarian crocodile long enough, the crocodile would eat them last.⁵

At the same time, there was little Roman influence on the lives of ordinary people. The settlement structure of hamlets and villages, and the fundamental techniques of farming and animal husbandry, remained relatively unchanged from the High Iron Age. It was mainly barbarian elites who adopted Roman customs, entered into clientship relationships with Roman authorities and otherwise exploited their Roman connections to their personal advantage.

One characteristic of the Roman provinces that did not cross into the barbarian world was urbanism in the form of agglomerations of population that served administrative, industrial and ceremonial functions. Examples of Roman urbanism stared barbarians right in the face along the frontier, from Noviomagus (modern Nijmegen in the Netherlands) to Aquincum (today's Budapest). These places flourished in the second and third centuries AD and were hearts of commercial and administrative activity for their hinterlands. Barbarians made no effort to imitate these urban communities, and the central places they established in parts of northern Europe were hardly urban in their structure. True urbanism in Europe beyond the Imperial frontier would have to wait until later in the first millennium BC.

Service in the Roman armies was an important social strategy for young barbarian men as well as being financially rewarding. Across northern Germany, Roman military items appear in male graves during the first two centuries AD.[6] These finds signify that the men had served in the Roman army and came home with enhanced status as a result. When they died, it was seen as important that this status be displayed with their bodies when they were buried.

In addition to mercenaries, what else did the Romans receive from the barbarians? For the most part, barbarian products did not leave much trace in the archaeological record. These include cattle, meat products, fish, goose quills, spices, honey, beeswax, fur, fleece and even, according to some, the hair of blonde maidens![7] Slaves, as always, were important commodities, especially since barbarian polities frequently fought each other and captured opponents who could be traded to the Romans. Baltic amber can be clearly sourced, and it flowed south to the frontier. Archaeologically, it may appear that more things from the Roman side crossed to the barbarian side, but in reality Roman goods were simply durable products like metals, pottery, coins and glass, while the barbarians traded in perishable goods.

Barbarians beyond the frontier zone

Outside the borderland zone of intense interaction between Romans and barbarians, some parts of northern Europe felt the impact of Rome's presence more keenly than others. Roman goods, weapons and ideas penetrated far into eastern and northern Europe during the first centuries AD, often brought back by natives of these areas after military service. Elsewhere, as in Ireland, Roman culture had little impact on High Iron Age society, although interesting developments occurred nonetheless, known through archaeology.

'Royal' sites in Ireland

During the final centuries BC and first centuries AD, Ireland served as an insular laboratory for the emergence of decentralized authority and elite status. Of particular importance are four Iron Age sites, traditionally termed 'royal' sites, that were taken up into Irish legend and myth as the seats of kings. The royal sites occupy prominent locations in the landscape and have very complex 'biographies' of construction and use that archaeologists are trying to untangle. They include Navan Fort (also known as Emain Macha) in Co. Armagh, Rathcrogan (also known as Cruachain) in Co. Roscommon, Dún Ailinne (also known as Knockaulin) in Co. Kildare, and Tara in the Boyne valley, Co. Meath. Some smaller sites, such as Cashel in Co. Tipperary, possibly served similar functions.

These four sites share several characteristics.[8] A large elevated area in the landscape, high enough to be called a 'hill' but certainly not a mountain, with a commanding view of the surrounding area, was enclosed with a bank and ditch. At Dún Ailinne the enclosed area covers 13 hectares (32 acres), while at Tara the interior of the enclosure is about 6 hectares (15 acres). In at least one case, Navan Fort, the ditch is inside the bank, suggesting that it had no defensive purpose. These locations had already been the scene of earlier ceremonial or mortuary activity. For example, the evocatively named 'Mound of the Hostages' at Tara is really a Stone Age passage tomb. In their interiors lie traces of multiple, overlapping circular enclosures, sometimes presenting themselves as 'figure-8' patterns. At Dún Ailinne, these were circular timber structures that increased in diameter over time, the largest being 43 metres (141 ft) across. Narrow passages and gates lead into them, so they have been interpreted as locations of ceremonial performances with access limited to the entitled.[9] A complex circular timber building was found in Navan Fort, consisting of five concentric rings of posts surrounded by an intricate exterior wall about 40 metres (130 ft) in diameter. This structure has been interpreted as an immense ceremonial roundhouse with a tall conical roof. It subsequently burned down and became covered by a huge mound.

Royal site at Dún Ailinne, Co. Kildare, Ireland, from the south. Top of hill is enclosed by a ditch.

Dating the Irish royal sites is very difficult, and it is still a bit hazy as to whether they all were in use concurrently. Navan Fort seems to have been the earliest, beginning in the middle of the first millennium BC. Even at this early date, it had long-distance connections and was a place to which gifts were brought, shown by the find of the skull of a Barbary ape (*Macaca sylvanus*) from North Africa dated to the fourth century BC. The animal bones from Navan Fort include twice as many pigs as cattle and many more pigs than sheep and goats, suggesting a collection associated with feasting. The ceremonial roundhouse was used briefly in the first century BC, but Navan Fort continued to be in use through the first century AD, perhaps later. Rathcrogan and Tara seem to have followed Navan Fort chronologically, and radiocarbon dating points to a span between the last two centuries BC and the second and third centuries AD. Dún Ailinne appears to be the last of these sites in use, with dates from the second century BC to the fifth century AD.

Whether or not they were literally 'royal', these large sites were clearly central places within the intertwined political and ritual

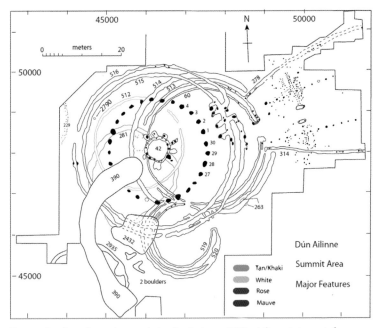

Composite plan of superimposed circular features at Dún Ailinne interpreted as ceremonial enclosures.

landscape of Iron Age Ireland. They share basic organizational principles and are on similar scales, but each differs from the others in details of its configuration, suggesting that there was room for local interpretation of shared ideology. Another question is, if these were locations of congregation and ceremony, where did people live? Archaeologists hope to figure out what these 'royal' sites meant to the communities that built them and how they relate to historical texts that mention them centuries later.

Veterans and merchants bring Rome to the Baltic

During the first centuries AD, High Iron Age societies flourished in southern Scandinavia and on the Baltic coasts of Poland and Lithuania. They continued along a developmental path from those described in the previous chapter, but even at this distance, Roman objects played a transformative role. In the borderland closer to the frontier, both mercantile trade and political actions accounted for widespread dispersal of Roman objects. By the third century

AD, a great wave of Roman products reached the Baltic shorelines and southern Scandinavia.

In many cases, these products are practical. Across northern Poland, over a thousand pieces of distinctive pottery, known as Samian ware, from workshops in Gaul and the Rhineland have been found.[10] Sometimes the distances that goods travelled are remarkable. For example, a type of metal cauldron made in the Meuse valley is called Vestland because they are abundant in that region of southwestern Norway.[11]

Once Roman coins got beyond the frontier zone, their function changed. Rather than serving as all-purpose money in mercantile transactions, coins played special roles as prestige objects. Although lower-denomination coins like silver denarii and bronze–brass sesterii may have continued to play a commercial role, they are frequently found in ceremonial or ritual contexts. Denarii occur in votive and war-booty offerings in southern Scandinavia, while in northeastern Poland sesterii were placed in the mouths of the dead in graves of the second century AD.[12] Gold coins such as solidi, introduced in the fourth century AD, were especially

One of over 100 wood-lined wells at Kwiatków, Poland, along the 'amber route' from the Baltic to Italy.

prized in the Barbarian World for socially or politically motivated payments, such as tribute, ransom, bridewealth and dowries and also blood money. Since they had ceased to have a face value as currency, gold coins were often melted down and refashioned into ornaments, including medallions called 'bracteates' and small gold 'figure foils'.

During the fourth and fifth centuries AD, solidi were especially in demand in Scandinavia. At Store Brunneby on the island of Öland, a hoard of seventeen solidi was found strewn across a field.[13] They were made between AD 394 and 451, dating their deposition to the second half of the fifth century AD. The Store Brunneby solidus hoard is only one of many deposits on Öland, along with others on Bornholm and Gotland, as well as on the Swedish mainland. Fischer writes of a 'gold haemorrhage' from the Western Roman Empire that arrived in Scandinavia with returning mercenaries.[14]

Amber from the Baltic coast was highly prized by Romans. Archaeologists have described an 'amber route' that led from areas in the eastern Baltic south through central Poland, through the Moravian Gate between the Carpathian and Sudeten mountains, and eventually reaching the Roman frontier on the Danube.[15] In reality the amber route was probably a wide corridor with many branches responding to demand from Roman jewellers, rather than a single trail. The collection of amber was probably managed by enterprising barbarians, but Pliny mentions a Roman soldier called Iulianus who travelled to the Baltic (or commissioned a traveller) to buy amber during the first century AD.[16] Other Romans followed, and locations such as Kalisia (identified as the modern Polish town of Kalisz) are noted on Ptolemy's map of Germania from the second century AD. Low-denomination Roman coins in graves and hoards across northern Poland are probably related to the amber trade.

Central places in the north

In southern Scandinavia, settlement complexes during the fourth and fifth centuries AD reflect integration greater than that seen in the clusters of High Iron Age farmsteads. Scandinavian archaeologists refer to these as 'central places' to indicate that multiple functions now converged in what was still essentially a rural settlement pattern.[17] Central places are not towns but rather 'localized geographies of settlement' that formed the focus of agricultural and craft production, sacred activities and prestige displays.

An important element in a central place was the residence of an individual of considerable authority and prestige called a 'magnate'.[18] The magnate was the dominant individual in the central place community whose manor was the largest and most impressive farmstead. Often it included a long timber hall for gatherings and ritual activities. Surrounding the magnate's estate were dependent farmsteads involved in craft production (especially metals) in addition to agricultural activities, as well as sacrificial and ritual sites, cemeteries and trading places. These activity places were scattered across the surrounding countryside rather than concentrated adjacent to the magnate's manor. Natural features structured the landscape into smaller units and connected the various elements.

Recognition of the growing overlap between religious activity and secular functions is key to understanding central places. While wetlands, groves, lakes, springs and other natural features continued to have spiritual significance, ceremonial activities also began to take place in and around structures, with the halls playing the role of cult buildings or shrines. Thus aristocratic power began to blend with religious authority rather than being a separate sphere of activity.

The beach market and magnate farm at Gudme

The extent to which Roman goods were pouring into the Barbarian World can be seen at Gudme, located on the eastern coast of the Danish island of Funen (Fyn). It lies along the shore of the Great Belt, a large strait through which maritime traffic from northern Germany passes on its way to the Kattegat. Around Gudme, settlements and cemeteries show the importance of this area between AD 200 and 600.[19]

Although finds had already been made around Gudme in the nineteenth century, including the Lundeborg gold hoard weighing over 4,200 grams (9 lb), archaeologists did not focus on this area until the 1980s. Metal-detector enthusiasts began turning up hundreds of gold, silver and bronze artefacts.[20] Open-minded archaeologists collaborated with them in serious archaeological investigation. Since metal-detectorists are compensated under Danish law for precious metals they discover, a lucrative arrangement was established. The sheer quantity of the finds showed that Gudme was a very special place, so archaeological investigations began in earnest.

The picture of life during the first half of the first millennium AD at Gudme has started to come into focus.[21] Gudme itself lies 5 kilometres (3 mi.) inland from Lundeborg on the coast, and the two formed a settlement complex and port between about AD 200 and 400, although it appears that the area was already becoming important during earlier centuries as shown by a cemetery at Møllegårdsmarken between Gudme and Lundeborg. For about 1 kilometre (½ mi.) along the coast near Lundeborg, near the mouth of a small brook that leads inland to Gudme, vast quantities of goods were delivered, many of which came from the Roman World. Some were broken during shipping and discarded, or simply lost. These include *terra sigillata* pottery and glass beads and rods, along with many Roman silver coins. Iron rivets from boats are also found in abundance, suggesting that boatbuilding and repairs were carried out. The Lundeborg coastal zone also included workshops for iron, silver and gold products as well as amber and bone carving.

One interpretation of Lundeborg is as a beach market, a sort of Iron Age Tesco or Wal-Mart where all sorts of goods were available, brought in from the south and picked up by the boatload to be dispersed to points around southern Scandinavia. Perhaps it had a seasonal or annual character rather than being a continuous operation. Lundeborg may be an early form of the emporia found across northern Europe later in the first millennium AD.

The exact relationship between the commercial activity on the coast and activities at Gudme inland is unclear, but with the help of the metal-detectorists, archaeologists have found a central settlement along with several outlying farmsteads. Of most interest

Outline of timber hall
at Gudme, Denmark,
showing massive interior
posts and smaller wall
posts outlined in white.

are several long timber structures, characterized as 'halls', which are much larger than the typical Iron Age longhouses of northern Europe. The largest, built in the second half of the third century AD and used for a number of decades, measured 47 metres (154 ft) long and 10 metres (33 ft) wide. The roof was supported by eight pairs of massive interior posts, creating three aisles along the length of the structure and a large open space in the middle. Nearby halls were smaller but equally robust in their construction.

Artefacts from the Gudme halls reflect wealth and privilege. Over a hundred Roman silver coins and pieces of gold jewellery were found among or in the postholes. Some of the ornaments originated from southeast Europe, while others were made locally, including a small face-effigy of a man and pieces of a silver neck ring highlighted with gold. Some were in votive deposits buried during the construction of the halls. Finds of gold and silver show where workshops were located in the Gudme complex. Much of this material was imported as cut-up scrap from the Roman World, including pieces of broken statues and dishes.

One of the products of these workshops was a home-grown Scandinavian form called a bracteate: a small disc of very thin embossed gold sheet. A small loop at the top suggests that they may have been worn as pendants or sewn on garments like a medal. Motifs are Nordic in character, either a human figure or face representing a personage or a god, or stylized horses, birds or spears. Metal-detectorists and chance finds in the Gudme area have turned up many more gold and silver deposits, marking it as one of the richest sites in northern Europe during the first centuries AD.

Gudme has been interpreted as the seat of a powerful magnate who could exert control over the surrounding farms and especially the beach market at Lundeborg, which in turn controlled the regional distribution of Roman goods. In many respects, this

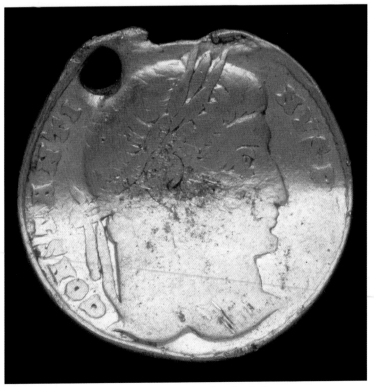

Roman gold coin perforated to make a pendant, found at Gudme.

arrangement seems comparable to the Hallstatt elites of central Europe and their control of the trade with the Greeks several centuries earlier. The question is whether Gudme was also a centre for religious activity, for the name itself means 'home of the gods'. An important lesson from Gudme and Lundeborg is the sheer quantity of Roman objects – coins, scrap gold and silver, pottery, glass – that were taken north and landed on a Danish beach 500 kilometres (300 mi.) from the Imperial frontier.

Uppåkra

The road from Malmö in southern Sweden goes up a gentle slope as it nears the edge of the university town of Lund. Open fields surrounding a small village on the top of this rise cover the site of one of the largest settlements in Scandinavia during the first millennium AD. Settlement at Uppåkra began during the first century BC and flourished over the next several centuries, and by AD 400 it probably had about 1,000 inhabitants. At its peak, Uppåkra covered about 400,000 square metres (100 acres). Several centuries of occupation left thick layers of archaeological deposits.[22]

Investigations at Uppåkra have flourished under another collaboration between amateur metal-detectorists and professional archaeologists. Over 20,000 metal artefacts have been plotted on the site plan to show their distribution. Most were bronze, but a significant number were iron, silver and gold. While many date to later phases of occupation, since they are closer to the surface and easier to detect, earlier ones have been found through excavations, which revealed a thriving community based on agriculture, trade and craft production.

The principal habitation unit at Uppåkra was the farmstead, of which there were around thirty to forty. They contained dwellings, barns, storage buildings and workshops. Craftsmen made high-quality objects from metals, bone and antler, as well as cloth and agricultural tools. Scales and weights indicate commercial activity, so we presume that Uppåkra functioned as a market town. Cattle were the primary livestock species, and barley was the principal crop, but archaeobotanical and archaeozoological evidence reflects a diverse subsistence economy. The soil in southern Sweden is very fertile, so Uppåkra and outlying settlements drew on a very productive agricultural system. Of particular note is the presence of plants prominent in Roman cuisine with a Mediterranean origin, such as dill and parsley, during the second century AD.[23]

One building at Uppåkra stood out.[24] It was not exceptionally large, but its construction and archaeological context made it clearly special. The structure measured 13.5 by 6 metres (44 × 20 ft), outlined by foundation trenches that were convex in plan on the longer sides. Gaps in the trenches indicated entrances. Inside, four immense postholes held thick timbers supporting a very high roof. In the centre was a large fireplace. Unravelling the soil layers in the trenches and the interior revealed that it had been built and rebuilt in seven stages, on the same general plan. It was in use for a very long time, having been first constructed around AD 200 and continuing until after AD 800. The location already had spiritual significance due to several earlier burial mounds nearby. Finely made objects like gold foils and exquisite metal and glass vessels, as well as deposits of intentionally destroyed weapons and bones of sacrificed animals and people, were found adjacent to the building. Abundant mouse droppings in the interior suggest that the building was not in everyday use but was only opened for special occasions.

Uppåkra represents another example of central place settlements that arose during the first millennium AD across northern Europe. Such localities were not *oppida* in the central and western European sense, since they do not have massive defensive structures, but they were nodal points for craft production, trade and ceremonial activity, which probably translated into regional authority and power. The Roman garden plants indicate that Uppåkra was on a network that brought them north. Perhaps its aristocracy demonstrated its status by consuming exotic Roman cuisine. After a long occupation, Uppåkra declined and was abandoned when political and religious authority converged nearby in Lund around AD 1000.

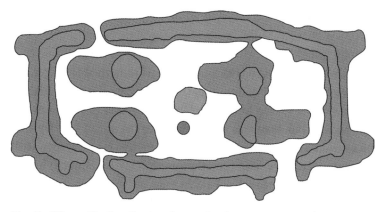

Ritual building at Uppåkra, Sweden, showing four large interior posts, the central hearth and trenches for exterior walls.

War-booty sacrifices

The war-booty sacrifice at Hjortspring described in the previous chapter was merely a warm-up to the widespread practice of offering weapons and associated military equipment in lakes and bogs across Scandinavia during the first centuries AD. Over 300 weapon sacrifices are known from Denmark alone, with more from Sweden and Norway. While it seems clear that these sacrifices were made by the victors using equipment of the vanquished, it is uncertain in most cases whether the victors were attacking or defending. At Hjortspring, the boat suggested that the defeated forces arrived from elsewhere.

Three boats were found in a bog at Nydam in southern Denmark in the nineteenth century, accompanied by an array of weapons and tools.[25] Two were made of oak and a third of pine. One of the oak boats was chopped up prior to deposition, while the other was flattened but complete.[26] Through tree-ring dating, the complete oak boat has been dated to AD 310–20, and it appears that the deposit was made two or three decades later. Based on the proportions of weapons, it seems that many Nydam warriors carried spears, but a third of them carried swords based on Roman designs. Archers represent a new element in barbarian forces, for several longbows of yew and hazel and many arrow shafts and arrowheads were found.

The oak boat from Nydam was more sophisticated in its construction than any described so far. It was built using a technique called clinker, in which overlapping strakes were fastened with iron rivets and caulked with wool cloth. This method is very much in the great Nordic boatbuilding tradition that reached its highest expression in Viking longboats later in the first millennium AD. The Nydam oak boat was also larger than the one at Hjortspring, measuring 23 metres (75 ft) long and 4 metres (13 ft) across, with fifteen pairs of oars. Two carved posts with stylized human heads, measuring about 1.4 metres (4½ ft) long, are interpreted as mooring posts that hooked over the gunwale.

About a century before the Nydam Boat and its associated weapons were sacrificed, an immense war-booty offering was made in Jutland in the valley of the river Å at Illerup.[27] Illerup Ådal A is the largest of several offerings here, dating to the beginning of the third century, about AD 210. It dwarfs other weapon deposits, containing 350 shields, 366 lances and 410 spears, over 100 swords, eleven sets of riding gear and many other items. There seems to have been no boat or archery equipment, however. The weapons

The restored Nydam Boat illustrating the 'clinker' construction technique, on display at the Archäologisches Landesmuseum, Gottorf Castle, Schleswig, Germany.

Reconstruction in the National Museum, Copenhagen, of the Nydam war-booty offering.

were systematically destroyed before being thrown into what was then a lake, either from boats or from the shore.

Of particular interest in the Illerup Ådal A deposit are bones of four horses with ritually inflicted injuries rather than everyday butchery marks.[28] Their deaths were caused by multiple concurrent blows from different types of weapons, suggesting that several people attacked them simultaneously. The horses are presumed to have belonged to the defeated army. Strontium isotope ratios show that they came from southern Scandinavia, indicating that the battle was a fairly local conflict rather than a trans-regional war.

Nonetheless, the combatants at Illerup Ådal A had distant connections, however indirect, with the Roman world at AD 200. Two hundred Roman silver coins, the most recent being from AD 187/8, were found in circumstances suggesting that they were carried in small pouches. Many of the swords at Illerup Ådal A were two-sided, pattern-welded models, made only in Roman workshops, although the hilts could have been added locally. Presumably these had been available to elite warriors.

The Illerup Ådal A weapons find and the Nydam Boat, separated by just over a century, show several important developments.

First, advances in boatbuilding technology in the Nydam oak boat reflect a dramatic improvement from that seen at Hjortspring and before. Second, the Illerup Ådal A deposit reflects a fighting force estimated to be about 400, five times larger than the 80 extrapolated from the Hjortspring deposit, while the Nydam finds indicate the incorporation of archers into the military unit. Ritual killing of horses at Illerup provides an equine parallel to the gruesome methods of dispatching the bog bodies. Finally, the Roman coins and swords at Illerup Ådal A show the penetration not just of isolated items but mass quantities of the products of Roman workshops and mints far into the Barbarian World, a good 650 kilometres (400 mi.) beyond the Imperial frontier.

People start moving

The middle of the first millennium AD is commonly seen as a time of great movement in the Barbarian World, which reached its apex from the fourth to seventh centuries. Barbarian peoples known from history, such as Goths and Vandals, roamed across the landscape in coherent groups, eventually penetrated the Roman frontiers, and wreaked havoc. They are conceptualized as roaring freight trains, with a locomotive of fierce warriors followed by wagons full of women, children and elderly who relocated en masse from their ancestral homes. Arrows on maps show their presumed routes across temperate and Mediterranean Europe. When they encountered Romans, things generally did not end well for the latter, enervated by the stresses of keeping control of a fracturing empire and unable to resist.

This image of the late Roman Empire resisting great barbarian migrations and eventually being overwhelmed has been a fixture in traditional scholarship and historical narrative since the sixteenth century.[29] Germanic invasions and conquests doomed the Roman Empire, and now form key elements in the origin stories of several modern European states. More recently, some scholars have begun to contest this view, leading still others to push back. Thus, historical studies of this period are awash in polemic and disagreement.

The main problem is that coherent mass movements of peoples between about AD 300 and 500 in the Barbarian World are virtually invisible in the archaeological record. We would expect to see distinctive artefact types and destroyed settlements marking horizons where violent barbarian bands passed through. Recall the penchant for war-booty sacrifices in the Barbarian World. Would not one expect marauding war bands from beyond the Roman frontier to continue this practice as they fought their way across Gaul and into the Mediterranean World? These are virtually unknown.

As a prehistoric archaeologist, I find this striking, since we do have opportunities to observe large-scale population movements in the archaeological record. The settlement of central Europe by farming populations during the sixth millennium BC is an example of migration and colonization in which communities practising agriculture have very different settlements, houses, artefacts and mortuary practices from the indigenous hunter-gatherer populations. We simply do not see similar discontinuities triggered by hypothesized mass population movements from the Barbarian World into the disintegrating Roman Empire during the first millennium AD.

The historian Peter Heather points out that people migrate for two basic reasons, both now and in the past: in search of opportunities that will give them and their families a better life, or because they were forced to move under threat of violence.[30] Guy Halsall has noted some general characteristics of migrations: population movement is rarely one-way; migrants follow established routes rather than flooding over the length of a border; migrants are drawn to pre-existing immigrant communities; and, most importantly, the flow of information is crucial to migration.[31] I would add that numbers of immigrants usually appear larger to the society being asked to absorb them than their absolute headcount. Many more people stay behind than migrate.

Movement of people throughout the Barbarian World was nothing new. It represented a continuation of interconnectedness and personal mobility reaching back to the Stone Age. The Amesbury Archer was well travelled, as was Egtved Girl. Ötzi was making a high-altitude crossing of the Alps. The difference now was movements of individuals and small groups were recorded by literate peoples with whom they had contact, who then aggregated these movements into narratives that described incursions of 'tribes' with collective identities. These narratives then shaped the views of their readership, as well as those of scholars in distant centuries who privilege written accounts over the archaeological record. Historians several centuries hence may presume that western Europe was overrun by bands of Polish plumbers in the early twenty-first century unless they understand the domestic political context in which this expression was used in France and Britain.

The inhabitants of the Barbarian World were agricultural peoples, as they had been for millennia. Agriculturalists often do relocate, but such relocation is largely at the level of individual households. Whole communities, particularly those who are enmeshed in a web of relationships with peer communities through trade, intermarriage and alliances, really do not pull up stakes collectively and resettle for the sake of moving. The barbarian peoples of western and northern Europe during the third, fourth and fifth centuries AD were not nomadic pastoralists, unlike the societies of the Eurasian steppes. It is indeed the case that some eastern populations made celebrated incursions into Europe, notably the Huns, but they are exceptions rather than the norm.

At the risk of offending scholars who are far more familiar with the written narratives, as an archaeologist, many migrations of the so-called Migration Period strike me both as attempts by literate ancient peoples to frame a narrative of changes they saw in their own society and as an academic construction formed through modern interpretations of textual sources. I realize that by taking this position I could be labelled a 'migration denier', but 'migration sceptic' might be more accurate. I do not deny that people moved around, but I suspect that these movements were not as collective, coherent and directed as the historical narratives assert. Disintegration of Roman authority, heightened awareness of cultural differences between the newcomers and Roman citizens, and congregation by immigrants in enclaves probably created an impression of movement on a larger scale and of greater coherence than actually occurred.

Rather than throwing the migration baby out with the bath-water,[32] however, let us examine some of the evidence for barbarian population movements during the final centuries of Roman authority in the West, with a focus on the Goths, Huns and Anglo-Saxons. In doing so, I will highlight where archaeology has provided insights into the nature of these movements and their consequences.

Faces in the crowd: the Goths

The Goths are the archetypal barbarians, so much so that there will be a separate book in this series devoted to them.[33] Their very name is scary and dark, so much so that it has been taken up by rebellious youth today (although there is no evidence that ancient Goths dressed only in black or used much eyeshadow). And they sacked Rome in AD 410, so they behaved like, well, barbarians. Let us, however, focus on the Goths before they emerged onto the pages of history, when they crossed the Imperial frontiers, rather than on their complex interactions with Roman authority.

Although they were mentioned by Tacitus and later by Ammianus Marcellinus, much of what we know about the early history of the Goths comes from an author named Jordanes. Jordanes was a sixth-century bureaucrat of the Eastern Roman Empire, who wrote *Getica* in the middle of the sixth century AD, drawing on a lost work by a Roman official named Cassiodorus who served in the court of Gothic king Theoderic at the turn of the fifth century AD. Cassiodorus is generally believed to have embellished, if not outright invented, his account of Gothic origins, and Jordanes, who had barbarian roots himself, repeated much of this already-dubious account.

As a result, even historians who normally would privilege writ-ten texts tend to discount much of Jordanes' writing, which places the location of the origin of the Goths in the Baltic region. This would have been solidly within the Barbarian World of the first several centuries AD, well beyond the Roman Imperial frontiers.

The lower Vistula drainage and surrounding areas seem to correspond to the area of Gothic origins if one swallows hard and takes Jordanes at face value. What does the archaeological record tell us was happening there during the first centuries AD?

Communities known to archaeologists as the Wielbark culture lived along the southern shore of the Baltic Sea during the first half of the first millennium AD, mainly along the lower Vistula. They are known mainly from cemeteries, which contain both cremation and skeletal burials outfitted with pottery and jewellery but no tools or weapons.[34] One such cemetery is at Rogowo in north-central Poland, associated with a settlement that covers about 6 hectares (15 acres) and contains 151 cremations and 137 flexed skeletal burials, many with bronze ornaments. Stable isotope analyses suggest that millet was a component of the diet alongside other terrestrial foods.

The communities of the Wielbark culture were at the northern end of the amber route. A key link in this route was a trackway that stretches nearly 1,200 metres (4,000 ft) across wetlands at Święty Gaj near the mouth of the Vistula river.[35] Built from oak logs, the Święty Gaj trackway was maintained for over three centuries, from the end of the first century BC to the early third century AD, and during this time it was widened from about 1.5 to 4 metres (5 to 13 ft) to accommodate increasing traffic to and from the amber-rich coastline of the eastern Baltic. Pieces of raw amber among the timbers clearly indicate the commodity being transported. If Roman merchants were involved, then Wielbark communities had some inkling about the things and practices of the distant Empire.

The evidence from Rogowo, Święty Gaj and other sites indicates that the Wielbark culture was a local development and that its communities did not arrive fully formed from elsewhere. Towards the end of the second century AD and perhaps again a century later, some members of Wielbark communities moved towards the southeast, eventually winding up north of the Black Sea in Ukraine. Archaeologists have associated pottery of the Cherniakhov culture with the Wielbark ceramic tradition. Przemysław Urbańczyk suggests that these were opportunistic social elites and their supporters, rather than entire communities.[36] Most of the inhabitants of the Wielbark region evidently stayed at home rather than face an uncertain future, since their cemeteries remained in use for several more centuries.

So, are the Wielbark and Cherniakhov societies early Goths migrating south from the Baltic before turning west to cause havoc in the Roman Empire? Historians are divided on this matter. Michael Kulikowski appears to take the position that because Jordanes' account is so suspect, any interpretation of the archaeological record that supports it is spurious.[37] Walter Goffart considers *Getica* to be a work of almost-fiction meant to serve an ideological purpose in the sixth century rather than to document actual events as historical fact.[38] Peter Heather seems inclined to give Jordanes the benefit of the doubt, while acknowledging the failings in his account, and believes the archaeological trail does lead back to the Baltic coast.[39]

Cemetery at Odry, northern Poland, dating to the second century AD, with circles of standing stones.

In the end, we simply do not know where Goths really came from, and even if we did, what form their migration took. It certainly does not seem to follow the traditional 'freight train' characterization. Instead, incremental relocations by elites and their retainers over many generations resulted in local peoples becoming entrained in a Gothic society. Eventually, like the other barbarian groups that enter history, the Goths became a loose confederation of tribal polities. By the time they show up within the Roman boundaries in the fourth century AD, they have become archaeologically invisible. This is not surprising, because as we have seen multiple times, the Imperial frontier was porous, and people identified as Goths had long since adopted a Roman lifestyle. Although the Goths fought the Romans on multiple occasions, the Romans also recruited them into their army.

In AD 376, many Goths sought refuge from the Huns along the southern Imperial frontier and were allowed to cross into the Empire. The Eastern Roman emperor Valens welcomed them at first but things soon turned sour, and in AD 378 an army of Goths routed the Roman army at Adrianople (modern Edirne in European Turkey) and killed Valens. This is considered the greatest defeat ever suffered by a Roman army. A fragile peace was made in AD 382, but from that point onward the Goths were loose cannons in the Roman World, always capable of organizing themselves and making trouble. The best example of this was Alaric, a leader of a group of Gothic auxiliary troops, who became dissatisfied, made demands, and was not paid for his services to both the Eastern and the Western Roman rulers. To show his dissatisfaction, he took his army into Italy and sacked Rome in August of AD 410.

By this point, Rome was no longer able to pick winners and losers and control the situation, and the Goths were neither its friends nor its enemies in any consistent way. During the fifth century AD, some Goths moved west to southern France and Spain, at which point they are called Visigoths, while Ostrogoths remained in southeastern Europe. Even the Goths had divided loyalties. Many Ostrogoths fought for Attila, while Visigoths fought against him. Some took up Christianity, which further divided them. Over time, any remaining identity these groups had as Goths faded, and they became assimilated into the societies that followed the collapse of the Roman Empire.

Huns: the notable exception

Allied propaganda during the First World War referred to Germans as 'Huns'. This is really a peculiar choice of barbaric epithet, for the Huns of the Barbarian World were anything but German. They represent a truly intrusive element during the fourth and fifth centuries AD, for they were steppe nomads from the interior of Asia. Metal cauldrons found in Hungary match those depicted in rock carvings on the Altai plateau between the steppes of Kazakhstan and the plains of Mongolia.[40] Their unexpected arrival in central Europe triggered a cascade of events that further disrupted barbarian societies along the Roman frontiers as well as imposing a high price on the Empire itself.

Resisted by China, the Huns headed west, crossing the Volga into Ukraine around AD 370. During the following decade, they overran or uprooted barbarian groups between the Don and the Dnieper. By the end of the third century, they had penetrated into the Carpathian Basin, threatening Roman Danubian provinces and sending shock waves through the southern tier of the Barbarian World in central Europe. Refugees flooded through the Imperial frontiers seeking refuge. By AD 425, Huns had moved the seat of their 'nomadic empire' to the Hungarian Plain and made themselves at home in the heart of Europe.

The character of the Huns' nomadic empire is debated by scholars. About 150 archaeological sites are known from the Carpathian Basin with distinctive Hunnic artefacts. The principal historical accounts are those of Priscus, a Greek emissary to the Huns in the middle of the fifth century AD and our friend Jordanes in the sixth century AD. One thing is clear: the nomadic character of the Hun way of life was completely novel to the sedentary Romans and their barbarian neighbours. Some scholars believe that the European Huns abandoned their nomadic life for a sedentary existence, living off tribute extorted from their neighbours. Others argue that the Huns continued to be mobile predators whose mounted archery skills terrified the peoples with whom they came into contact during the first half of the fifth century AD.[41]

The Hun empire reached its zenith under Attila, who ruled between AD 444 and 453 from multiple timber palaces rather than a single permanent capital. In AD 445, Attila made a foray across the Alps and down into Italy before turning back and then planned and abandoned a siege of Constantinople in the following years. In AD 451, Attila turned west and struck across the Rhine into the heart of Gaul. It is amazing how far he got before a force consisting of Romans and Visigoths confronted him outside Châlons. Mutual slaughter ensued. Although the victory of the Roman–Visigoth coalition was by no means decisive, Attila withdrew to the Carpathian Basin, where he died two years later. Political infighting and revolts by subjugated peoples ended the Huns' unity, and after a defeat in Pannonia in AD 455, they retreated back to Ukraine and to the steppes beyond.

The Huns' incursion into central Europe is illuminating in that it shows what real barbarian predation on the decaying Roman Empire could look like. Most other barbarian movements, in my view, were less predatory and more parasitic: 'inside jobs' in which migrant streams were drawn to enclaves of brethren who had been in Roman service. Sometimes these groups formed war bands to expand their power and territorial appropriation at the expense of Roman authority. Huns, on the other hand, were highly organized, coherent and motivated, but not inclined to capture and hold territory when opposed by equal forces. They filled a geopolitical vacuum that emerged in the Carpathian Basin between the western and eastern parts of the Roman Empire, while most barbarian movements (in my view) filled local vacuums in areas of Roman authority and military control.

The Huns, however, triggered non-economic movements of people who feared for their lives. As such, they dislodged people who otherwise might not have been inclined to move. The pressure and instability pushed the Visigoths westward at the end of the fourth century AD and provoked groups from southern Germany to seek refuge within the Roman frontiers.

The advent of the Saxons

In eastern England, collapse of Roman authority brought migrants from Germania Magna during the early fifth century AD. These were the Anglo-Saxons, whose arrival is portrayed by chroniclers like Gildas and Bede as a momentous event, the 'Adventus Saxonum', and archaeologically is seen in the appearance of Germanic artefacts and characteristic cemeteries by the middle of the fifth century.[42] The arrival of the Anglo-Saxons is one of the better-documented migrations of this period, but there is still considerable scholarly debate about its character. The chroniclers portray it as a massive invasion that replaced the local population. Scholars have recently questioned this replacement hypothesis and argued that smaller Anglo-Saxon groups migrated to England as part of the overall turmoil of the time, with native Romano-British communities continuing largely unaffected, or that changes were the result of *in situ* developments with a minimal outside contribution.[43]

West Stow on the river Lark in eastern England was a typical Anglo-Saxon settlement occupied between the early fifth and the mid-seventh centuries AD.[44] Excavations at West Stow revealed semi-subterranean houses, a very Continental house type, clustered around several small timbered structures known as halls. The population of West Stow consisted of three or four families at any one time. Animal bones from the earliest Anglo-Saxon houses at West Stow indicate that alongside cattle, sheep and goats, there was a dramatic upswing in the use of pigs, which might be a signal of a colonizing population interested in high meat production.[45] As time went on, the proportion of pigs settled back down. Aside from the temporary spike in pigs, however, subsistence practices at West Stow do not indicate marked changes from Romano-British practices. Either the Anglo-Saxon arrival had little impact on native communities or the immigrants adopted the local system of animal husbandry.

Strontium isotope ratios of nineteen individuals from an early Anglo-Saxon cemetery at Berinsfield in Oxfordshire have been analysed.[46] Most were born locally, consumed food grown on local soils and drank local water. Four, however, may have grown up elsewhere. One male, buried with a Roman belt fitting, has strontium ratios that do not fit those found in England and are a closer match to ones in southwest Germany. Another has non-local ratios that might be found in interior Germany, but could also be from northeastern England. Two others have strontium ratios that are not local but which fall within the values for other parts of southern Britain. The data from Berinsfield do not seem consistent with massive population replacement by Anglo-Saxon invaders and point either towards small-group migration and intermingling with indigenous communities or native adoption of Anglo-Saxon cultural expression.

The bees in the tomb

Out of Germania Magna came the Franks, whose name derives from that of a throwing axe, the *francisca*, now preserved in the name of the country of France. They first attracted Roman attention in the third century AD as an alliance of tribes between the Rhine and the Weser, and during the fourth century AD they crossed the Roman frontiers to cause havoc before settling in northern Belgium and taking up Roman ways. After that, they were very loyal to Rome and teamed up with the Romans and Visigoths to defeat the Huns in AD 451.

The first Frank to step into history was Childeric, their ruler in the third quarter of the fifth century AD. At first, he was one of several Frankish kings in the wake of the decline of Roman authority. Childeric died in AD 481 or 482 and was buried at Tournai, in Belgium along the border with France.[47] His grave was discovered in 1653 and despite clumsy excavation, revealed an elaborate burial clearly intended to substantiate the power of his heir, Clovis. A gold signet ring in a Roman style with an inscription, CHILDERICI REGIS, identified the body as Childeric. Multiple horse burials, at least thirty, were found nearby, suggesting an even more exotic mortuary practice, echoing that seen in Scythian tombs on the steppes.

Of special significance are the carefully chosen coins in Childeric's tomb, which represent five centuries of coinage intended to demonstrate dynastic legitimacy recognized by both the vestiges of Roman authority and competing barbarian kings.[48] The coin collection, fortunately recorded in detail before being stolen in the nineteenth century, included 89 gold solidi minted by highly regarded emperors. Other gold objects included 300 little bees with *cloisonné* infilling that adorned Childeric's cloak. Seeking to wrap himself in ancient royal history, Napoleon Bonaparte also had his coronation robe ornamented with gold bees.

The Frankish royal dynasty that emerged with Childeric is known as the Merovingians. Although their story lies outside the scope of this book, the Franks and their Merovingian rulers illustrate the convergence of Germanic barbarian and Gallo-Roman cultural elements amid competition for authority in the post-Roman era. Fifth-century AD Frankish burials, such as those at the cemetery at Saint-Aubin-des-Champs in Normandy, contain grave goods that include ceramic vessels, glass vessels and metal ornaments and weapons,[49] reflecting the broad territorial integration under their rulers. In recent centuries, the Merovingian dynasty, as interpreted by generations of historians and archaeologists, has been a foundation of French national identity.

Sandby Borg

The Barbarian World ended at many times and places, while elsewhere it continued forward into history, like tracks in a railway yard in which some sidings end at bumpers while others continue on to rejoin the main line. One of these tracks ended on the shore of the Baltic Sea on the island of Öland at the end of the fifth millennium BC. Here, a ringfort lies about 42 metres (140 ft) from the current waterline. One spring day around AD 480, something very bad happened at Sandby Borg.[50]

Sandby Borg is one of nearly twenty ringforts from the first half of the first millennium AD on Öland. It is a stone oval about 92 metres (300 ft) along its long axis, with walls 4 metres (13 ft) wide at the base. Inside were 54 stone and turf buildings with gravel and limestone floors, with houses in the centre and stables and storehouses around the inside of the wall. A well provided water.

Reconstruction of an Anglo-Saxon village at West Stow, Suffolk, showing both semi-subterranean houses and timber halls.

In 2010, archaeologists noticed evidence of unauthorized digging and moved to secure the site. Metal-detectorists were mobilized to locate metal objects, and exploratory excavations commenced. The results were astonishing. Lying under a thin cover of soil, at least ten skeletons bore traces of violent deaths and had been left unburied where they fell. Eventually, the turf house walls collapsed and covered their remains. One skeleton of an individual in his late teens had a massive lethal cut to the skull which could only have been made if he had been kneeling. Lamb bones, the remains of uneaten meals, indicate that the slaughter took place in the spring. Archaeologists believe that dozens of additional skeletons lie across the ringfort's interior.

The attackers looted the site, but they missed five caches of beads and jewellery hidden just inside the doorways of separate houses. These included gold and silver brooches in a Germanic style, bells, gold rings and amber and glass beads. A gold solidus from the reign of Valentinian III (assassinated in AD 455) provides evidence of returning mercenaries, as do the glass beads.

Who attacked Sandby Borg? Although the ringfort lies in an indefensible location near the shore, archaeologists believe that the attackers were fellow residents of Öland. As wealth was accumulated in farmsteads, it drew the attention of marauding gangs that preyed on fellow islanders. One day, the alarm was raised, and the inhabitants of nearby farmsteads sought refuge in Sandby Borg. In anticipation that some would not survive, they hid their valuables, presumably in prearranged locations. It was to no avail, and they were all slaughtered.

Sandby Borg was never reoccupied, unlike other ringforts on Öland that saw habitation in later centuries. It may have remained off-limits, first as a place of violent death, then perhaps as a haunted or taboo location. In many respects, the Sandby Borg massacre encapsulates many conditions at the end of the Barbarian World in which wealth coming over long distances triggered local social stresses that often ended badly.

The Barbarian World in AD 500 and beyond

Ending this book in AD 500 imposes an artificial stopping point on the continuous story of the Barbarian World, and thus the heading includes the words 'and beyond'. The societies of temperate Europe

Gold-and-glass bees from the coat of Childeric.

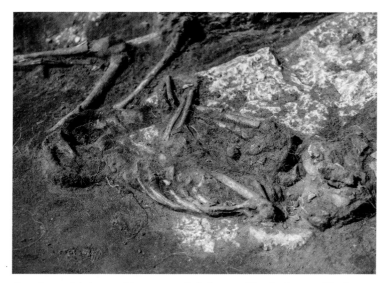

One of several skeletons of the massacred inhabitants of Sandby Borg on Öland.

did not stop changing, and the impact of the Roman Empire was permanent, even if it had ceased to function in western Europe. Barbarian peoples were now left to their own devices and gradually developed the characteristics of civilization on their own. The artificial boundary between the peoples and places that lay within the Roman frontiers and those outside of it disappeared, and the remaining parts of the Barbarian World became integrated with the peoples of Gaul and Britain just as before the Romans arrived.

The dominant feature of post-Roman temperate Europe was the emergence of many small kingdoms. Most had limited territorial aims but provided vehicles for the aggrandizement of their rulers and their retinues. The heterarchical structures of the High Iron Age faded in favour of hierarchical organization and dynastic succession. Some of these kingdoms grew over time to control large areas. The Franks, now led by Childeric's son Clovis, consolidated control over northern Gaul and neighbouring parts of Germania.

Across the Barbarian World, we see changes in ritual behaviour. For example, in southern Scandinavia the practice of depositing valuables in bogs and wetlands ends around AD 500. After that, such items appear mainly at the seats of local magnates and in ritual structures, like the halls at Gudme and Uppåkra. This transfer of sacred activities from wild locations to central places of habitation and commerce presaged religious transformations of the second half of the first millennium across northern Europe.

Christianity, the dominant religion in the Roman Empire since the fourth century, was taken up in neighbouring parts of the Barbarian World. Missionaries from Roman Britain and perhaps Gaul, as exemplified by Patrick (although he was certainly not the first), brought Christianity to Ireland early in the fifth century, and by AD 500 it was firmly established. The penetration of Christianity into southern Scandinavia and eastern Europe took a couple more centuries, but it was on the way. A dramatic instance of the acceptance of Christianity by a prominent barbarian was the conversion of Clovis in AD 496.

Many Roman towns were abandoned during the fifth century AD. Londinium, whose defensive walls survived and where ruins of Roman buildings were probably still visible, appears to have been largely depopulated. Instead, rural populations continued to live in farmsteads, hamlets and small villages, as they had done for centuries. We do not see great agglomerations of population in temperate Europe at the middle of the first millennium AD, although central places like Uppåkra continued to flourish and grow. Although the supply of Roman goods and coins faded, trade in commodities and slaves continued to motivate inter-regional connections throughout temperate Europe.

The next 500 years would see the revival of towns, the emergence of trading ports around the North Sea and Baltic Sea, the flourishing of the Merovingian and Carolingian Dynasties in western Europe, and the introduction of Christianity to eastern Europe and Scandinavia. From the eighth century AD onward, the dominant force of coastal temperate Europe was a people known as Vikings, who were responsible for the establishment of many towns like Dublin across western Europe, as well as penetrating into eastern Europe and establishing the Russian state. The Vikings are often considered to be the last barbarians because of their unfortunate habit of sacking coastal settlements and looting monasteries, but their peaceful activities such as exploration and commerce are their more lasting legacy. But they did not come out of the blue. The Vikings, along with the other societies of the early Middle Ages in temperate Europe, were products of millennia of prehistoric development. The roots of European civilization can be found as much in the Barbarian World as in the classical civilizations of Greece and Rome.

SIX

BARBARIANS
LIVE ON

The barbarians of prehistoric Europe exercise a powerful hold on the imagination of the twenty-first century. This fascination is not new, however, and much of the way modern people view the prehistoric past is based on perceptions, appropriations and myths that emerged long ago. The word 'barbarian' is casually thrown about to refer to anyone who engages in violent, uncivilized behaviour. This is a legacy of the Greek and Roman portrayals of the non-literate inhabitants of temperate Europe and the exalted position of texts by classical authors in humanistic scholarship that began in the Renaissance. Barbarians are permanently consigned to a subordinate status as depraved and culturally deprived *Untermenschen* until they were illuminated by language, culture and civility coming from the Mediterranean.

In many cases, such as in fantasy literature, video games and film, the depravity of barbarians is portrayed in the most lurid fashion, not just behaving viciously but also having fantastic powers and implausible mystical insights. Conan, a character invented by pulp fiction writer Robert E. Howard (1906–1936) for fantasy stories in the 1930s, is perhaps the most celebrated depiction of a barbarian in this light. He is said to be from Cimmeria, a fictional homeland whose name evokes the label that Herodotus gave to barbarian tribes northeast of the Black Sea, although Howard imagines him as having 'pre-Celtic' roots. In his original conception, Conan speaks many languages, is capable of profound observations and possesses immense strength. Howard created an imagined Barbarian World in which Conan has his adventures. Unfortunately, in more recent depictions, Conan has become a simpler brute, in keeping with the 'barbarian' stereotype.

On one hand, an accurate imagining of the Barbarian World must include its endemic violence that was simply a fact of life in prehistoric Europe. There was clearly also a mystical, spiritual side to barbarian life, as shown by practices such as votive deposits and war-booty offerings. The inter-regional connectedness of local societies meant that it would not be out of the question for a leader to be able to communicate in several dialects. So the original Conan genre is not that wide of the mark in certain aspects. On the other hand, the recent indelible association among Conan/ Schwarzenegger/Austrian accent/gratuitous bloody violence/ supernatural characters has done the Barbarian World a disservice.

Archaeology is a field of scholarship in which popular imagination confronts evidence and reasoned interpretation. While this might be common to all historical disciplines, archaeology has the added mystery of lacking historical individuals with biographies supported by primary sources. Thus we see an explosion of theories and narratives surrounding Ötzi the Iceman, as people try to turn him into a historical figure. Arminius has a name and an event associated with his life, but yet an immense mythology has built up around him. After the fall of Rome, more barbarians leave prehistory and enter the historic world, but they are beyond the scope of this book. For most of prehistory, the lack of historic figures means that all sorts of stories can be imagined, whether or not they conform to evidence (or lack thereof). The attraction of Conan is that despite being fictional, he is a character with a name, an origin, and a story, however implausible.

A usable past

It would be sad if Conan was our only way of connecting with the Barbarian World. Luckily, there are many other ways in which the barbarians of prehistory are present in the consciousness of the modern world. The Barbarian World looms large in European culture and society. Continuity from prehistory into medieval history and thence the history of more recent centuries means that there is no fracture between prehistory and history as there is in the New World. The prehistoric societies can be incorporated into a narrative that reaches back at least to the end of the Ice Age that modern Europeans and their descendants can consider part of their own story.

The American historian Henry Steele Commager (1902–1998) has pointed out the difference between the American view of its past as a literary exercise in either celebration or sentimentality about documented events and characters and the European past rooted in folklore, oral tradition and myth.[1] Both represent a search for a 'usable past' that helps people understand who they are and to create a communal understanding in the present. For Europe, the Barbarian World is very much a part of its usable past.

The construction of such a usable past inevitably involves simplification and certainty. Unfortunately, the archaeological record is complicated, incoherent and conflicted. All narratives based on it, like this book, are selective, in the way that a drawing differs from a photograph. In the former, the artist chooses what to show and what to omit, while a photograph is faithful to what the eye sees, although in the hands of a skilled photographer it too can be manipulated. To take this analogy a step further, a caricature is a drawing that emphasizes certain characteristics of the subject to make a point. The transformation of the Barbarian World into a usable past in the public imagination requires it to be transformed into a caricature, not only to simplify a complicated body of information but also to exaggerate or even misrepresent some key aspects to make a point deemed useful for a modern audience. In the public imagination, the Barbarian World is a palimpsest of caricatures rooted in selective appropriation of the archaeological record.

Some caricatures of barbarian life are literally cartoons, a common way for modern people to encounter the ancient world for the first time. Archaeologists enjoy cartoons about the people they study. My undergraduate mentor at the University of Pennsylvania, Bernard Wailes (1934–2012), had a display of them on his office door. Unfortunately, too many cartoons about prehistoric people show them in the company of dinosaurs, an anachronism of about 100 million years. Another common motif is the cave dweller who has just chipped a wheel out of stone. The reader of this book knows that the first wheels were made from wood during the fourth millennium BC, so the sheer improbability of a stone wheel does not reflect well on prehistoric mastery of materials.

Although not well known in the New World, the comic character Astérix has had perhaps the most durable impact of a barbarian on cartoon readership in Europe. Astérix and his pal Obelix are Gauls living in northwestern France who resist the Roman invaders together with their fellow villagers. The Astérix comics were first written by René Goscinny (1926–1977) and illustrated by Albert Uderzo nearly sixty years ago.[2] Although the humour is distinctly Gallic, the Astérix series has been translated into many languages and remains wildly popular throughout Europe. For many young people, especially in France, Astérix is their first contact with the Barbarian World.

As a guide to life in the Barbarian World, however, the Astérix comics should not be taken too seriously. In 2011 an exhibition called 'Les Gaulois' at the Cité des Sciences in Paris was devoted to debunking the image of High Iron Age life portrayed in Astérix. It noted that rather than being pugnacious forest dwellers, Gauls were a refined, complex society, living in towns and villages, with sophisticated agriculturalists and stockbreeders, skilled metalworkers and participants in interregional trading networks. Astérix comics are rife with anachronisms. The menhirs, or standing stones, that Obelix carves and erects really date to the Stone Age. Yet, they would have still been visible in the landscape of the first century BC, as they are still today.

At the same time, archaeologists must suppress their sense of umbrage when they see their beloved prehistoric world portrayed this way. Astérix is only a comic, and its humour is topical within its modern context, not a prehistoric one. In an account of the 'Les Gaulois' exhibit,[3] archaeologist Matthieu Poux of the University of Lyon was quoted as saying that the Astérix comics are 'a kind of synthesis of the positive values of contemporary society and of the imaginary world created by Antiquity'. This is the essence of 'a usable past'.

Reconstructed Village Gaulois in the shadow of a giant radar dome at Pleumeur-Bodou in Britanny evokes an imagined prehistoric world in which Astérix had his adventures.

The perception of time

The greatest source of confusion in the public perception of the prehistoric past is time. If a century seems like a long time to someone, then a millennium will be ten times more difficult to comprehend. Extending the timescale back several millennia, the difficulty in understanding the tempo of prehistoric life increases logarithmically. Archaeologists are accustomed to working over such long spans of time, and they often lose sight of the fact that non-archaeologists find them hard to comprehend. The Stone Age does not seem much earlier than the reign of Augustus in the eyes of many. I call this phenomenon the 'telescoped past' in which the Stone Age, Bronze Age and Iron Age are compressed into a single 'antiquity'.

We encounter this telescoping of the past in the assignment of the symbols of one era to the iconography of another, which in turn is appropriated by modern culture. For example, spiral ornaments pecked into the lintels and kerbstones of Stone Age passage graves are portrayed as a 'Celtic' motif in modern art, design and

Modern park in Philadelphia devoted to Irish immigration displays motifs that derive from both megalithic and La Tène styles, each point in time separated by millennia.

advertising, despite occurring several millennia before any peoples that could be called by that name.

The classic example of time-transgressive appropriation, to put a fancy name on it, involves Stonehenge. As we saw in Chapter One, Stonehenge is a Stone Age monument. It really has no primary connection with the priestly class known as Druids from Roman accounts. Yet modern seekers have telescoped prehistory to appropriate both the Druids and Stonehenge in a single imagined antiquity, despite their separation in prehistory by two millennia. Such a telescoping of the archaeological record seems normal to many people who do not share the archaeologist's keen sense of time and change.

Other examples of such telescoping of millennia are not as well known, but they are ubiquitous where a myth can be attached to a site or monument. On a mountain called Knocknarea in northwest Ireland, a massive unexcavated Stone Age passage grave dated to the fourth millennium BC is named Queen Meave's Tomb after a mythical warrior queen of Irish legend. Meave is certainly not buried in the tomb, if she even existed, but the fusion of physical traces of the past with the more recent myth has given the site a composite identity. Archaeologists themselves refer to the tomb as 'Meave', preferring to adapt to the modern usage rather than assert their understanding that the passage grave has nothing to do with a Celtic queen.

Barbarians in the media

Archaeological discoveries have always made for a good story. The *Neue Zürcher Zeitung* newspaper frequently covered Keller's 1854 discoveries of the Swiss lake settlements, and Keller in turn made sure that the press became aware of his latest finds and his theories about the form of the pile dwellings. Excavations at Biskupin were described in the Polish press as the 'Polish Pompeii' during the 1930s, and visits of leading Polish politicians and clergy to the excavations were widely publicized. I have a folder full of press clippings about excavations my colleague Ryszard Grygiel and I conducted at the Stone Age sites of Brześć Kujawski and Osłonki in Poland. We were periodically visited by a local reporter and made sure we had a good story for him.

Archaeology was a subject made for the era of glossy, mass-market magazines. The *Illustrated London News* routinely featured the archaeology of Europe. Many articles were illuminated by the artwork of Alan Sorrell (1904–1974), perhaps the foremost archaeological illustrator of the mid-twentieth century, who took field observations and drawings and brought them to life.[4] His bird's-eye views of Maiden Castle show the complexity of the fortification system. *National Geographic* today is continuing the tradition of lavishly illustrated articles about archaeology and is finally paying attention to the Barbarian World, with articles about Ötzi, Stonehenge and other discoveries in temperate Europe.

Since archaeology inherently has visual interest, the golden days of radio did not do much to promote it. It was not until the advent of television after the Second World War that archaeology found a new medium for generating public interest. In 1951, the director of the University Museum at the University of Pennsylvania in Philadelphia, Froelich Rainey (1907–1992), began to host a show entitled *What in the World?* On this show, a mysterious archaeological or ethnographic object of unknown function was presented to a panel of experts, drawn from the Penn community of archaeologists and anthropologists, who tried to figure out what it was and its cultural context.[5] It ran for about fifteen years and was my first exposure to archaeology growing up in Philadelphia.

The success of *What in the World?* became known in the international archaeological community and inspired *Animal, Vegetable or Mineral?* which made its debut on the BBC in 1952. It was hosted by Cambridge archaeologist Glyn Daniel (1914–1986), but it made its frequent guest Sir Mortimer Wheeler (1890–1976) a star, such that he was named the British 'Television Personality of the Year' in 1954.[6] With his upturned moustache, military bearing and witty repartee, Wheeler was a telegenic natural who went on to appear on other archaeology shows during the 1950s.

After a relative absence of several decades, archaeology again seems everywhere on television. Channels such as National

Geographic and Discovery feature archaeology prominently in their programming. *Time Team*, in which archaeologists excavated a site per episode, ran for almost twenty years on Britain's Channel 4. The latest discoveries at Stonehenge are always good for an hour of programming, and Ötzi appears from time to time when a new theory about his death is publicized. Most shows benefit from the advice of professional archaeologists, who have methodological and interpretive standards and who often become media personalities themselves.

Sir Mortimer Wheeler, star of *Animal, Vegetable or Mineral?*

An archaeological event that routinely makes the news is the celebration of the winter solstice at Newgrange. Unlike Stonehenge, where the summer solstice has been appropriated by neo-druids, the winter solstice observance at Newgrange is a more straight-forward recognition that its Stone Age builders incorporated an astronomical alignment into the tomb. Many people gather around its fake limestone facade to wait for dawn. Only a few can fit inside for the full effect of the rising sun shining down the passage at 8.58 a.m. A free annual lottery is held to determine the lucky ones.[7] Actually, this effect can be observed from 18 to 23 December, and winners are chosen for each of six mornings from over 30,000 entries. Unfortunately, this being Ireland in winter, the possibility of the sun shining down the passage is never certain. Even if it is not possible to be inside, the feeling of waiting in darkness, as people had done in the Stone Age, for the longest night of the year to end must be very powerful.

Barbarians serve the state

An important role of archaeology in modern society, of which the public is rarely aware, has been its mobilization for the creation of a common national identity and providing legitimacy to leaders and their policies. Archaeologists are generally uncomfortable with this appropriation of their discipline. Over the last century, some have resisted actively while others made careers under state patronage, but most have tried to ignore it and keep on doing their research and scholarship. Yet unbeknownst to most of the public, archaeological monuments, sites and finds have often been turned into symbols that then become manipulated to fit a political agenda. Only recently have archaeologists taken a reflective look at how their discipline has been used to legitimize narratives of national origins and territorial claims.

Napoleon III (1808–1873), emperor of France from 1852 to 1870, was the first national leader to realize the potential of archaeology. He sought to create a national identity that was linked to both Gauls and Romans. This would not be a simple task. The Gauls, resisting a foreign invader, would seem a natural candidate to be the heroes, but historical France owes its language, culture and institutions to the Romans, so they were also good guys in the end. It was not a simple 'us versus them' or a heroic defeat by an oppressor. So Napoleon III chose three of the *oppida* mentioned by Caesar and turned them into symbolic focal points.[8] The three – Alésia, Bibracte and Gergovia – were linked by association with Vercingetorix and his struggles with Caesar in 52 BC. At Bibracte, Vercingetorix was chosen to lead the confederation of several tribes; at Gergovia, he was victorious; and at Alésia he was defeated by Caesar.

Alésia was the site chosen for the most intense investment. Napoleon III commissioned excavations with generous financial support, and in 1865, a statue 6.7 metres (22 ft) high of Vercingetorix by Aimé Millet was erected on an elaborate pedestal designed by the famous architect Viollet-le-Duc. Flowery dedications linked Napoleon III to Vercingetorix, who was elevated to the stature of a patriot. At the same time, Caesar's conquest, the triumph of civilization over barbarism, was invoked to support French colonialism in Africa and the Pacific. The physical substantiation of the past and its monumentalization at Alésia fused the two messages: Gauls as resisters and Romans as civilizers, the combination of which formed the French national identity.

Gergovia and Bibracte also saw excavations sponsored by Napoleon III, but their transformation into sacred places came later. The sudden end of the Second Empire in the Franco-Prussian War of 1870 derailed this project. After things settled down, the role of these sites in the national collective memory was transformed from the complicated tension between Gallic resisters and Roman civilizers to a simple nationalist ideology of resisting foreign invaders – in this case, Germans. At Gergovia, a monument to Vercingetorix was not erected until 1900 and, by then, the only collective memory was of defeat and a desire for revenge. A statue of Joan of Arc, who also resisted foreign occupiers, was added to that of Vercingetorix at Alésia, in case anyone did not get the message.

Around the same time that Vercingetorix was being elevated to national hero in Napoleon III's attempt to create a national origin myth, similar developments were taking place in Germany. Just as the Romans were central to the French narrative, they also played

Monumental statue of Vercingetorix by Aimé Millet on Mont Auxois, Burgundy,
France.

a leading role in the German one. The difference was that in France, the Romans eventually won and illuminated the defeated but noble Gauls with their civilization; in Germany, the Romans were defeated soundly and their expansion halted. Central to this narrative was the slaughter in the Teutoberg Forest of Varus and his legions by Arminius, where the Romans were definitely the bad guys, and the Germans won.

By the nineteenth century Arminius had been renamed Hermann, a mistranslation sometimes attributed (although this is disputed) to Martin Luther. Nationalists in nineteenth-century Germany, divided into many states such as Bavaria and Prussia, adopted Hermann as a representative of their shared ancestry.[9] After all, Arminius/Hermann formed a coalition of tribes to defeat the Romans. Moreover, the French rhetoric about their Roman origins played into this, since it enabled the Germans to draw a distinction between themselves and Napoleonic France, which was of course destined for defeat just like Varus.

Following this complex web of associations is a challenge, and it is not necessarily coherent, but it provides some early examples of the Barbarian World being used centuries later to construct a usable past for the advancement of national(ist) goals. For the time being, these goals were symbolic and did not involve world domination. The First World War provided another impetus to such projects, and like many of its unanticipated consequences, begins the next episode in which the archaeology of the Barbarian World was saddled with the purpose of authenticating historical claims.

By this time in Germany, the archaeologist Gustaf Kossinna (1858–1931) had achieved prominence. Today, Kossinna is definitely not seen as a good guy, whereas in his time, his general approach to archaeology was not much different from that of his contemporaries.[10] He saw diagnostic artefacts of distinctive types and styles as markers of collective affiliation within a particular region. Kossinna's research focused on the borderlands between Germans and Slavs, mostly during the first millennium AD. Certain artefacts identified Germans, while others were markers of the Slavs. Trade and other forms of connectivity were not taken into account. Today, we would not draw such simplistic equivalencies, but in the first decades of the twentieth century, this was mainstream archaeological thinking.

Where Kossinna went off the rails was in his insistence on sharp and impermeable boundaries between cultural groups that persisted into historical times. This view played right into the hands of nationalists seeking authentication of claims to land in the east, on the principle that once an area was inhabited by Germans, Germany as a nation had a perpetual claim on that territory. Kossinna was sympathetic to such thinking, and in popular writings expressed nationalist opinions openly. His identification of ancient Germanic artefacts at sites in the Vistula drainage supported his opinion that this region should belong to Germany in the twentieth century. Moreover, he considered the ancient and modern Germans culturally superior to the peoples who lived to the west and the east of them.

Kossinna died in 1931, and within two years, Adolf Hitler and the Nazi Party had taken control in Berlin, beginning perhaps the closest connection ever between archaeologists and a national government to promote and authenticate an official view of the past.[11] The archaeologists involved were a mix of disciples of Kossinna and others who saw career opportunities in the new order. Typically, the Nazi regime set up two separate archaeological operations, one under the auspices of Party ideologist Alfred Rosenberg (1893–1946) and the other within the empire led by Reichsführer-ss Heinrich Himmler (1900–1945). Both had the same goal: the legitimation of the mythical narrative of a German ethnic and racial identity with prehistoric roots and eventually authentication of prior German presence in conquered lands.

The main archaeologist in Rosenberg's office was Hans Reinerth (1900–1990), successor to Kossinna in Berlin. Reinerth was the excavator of the Bronze Age waterside settlement of Wasserburg Buchau, mentioned in Chapter Two. He received the title of Reich Deputy for German Prehistory and oversaw the Confederation for German Prehistory, which promoted archaeology to support German racial theories and patriotic fervour. Rosenberg had some ideas of his own about prehistory, including a theory that Germanic peoples originated from a lost Atlantic island, a Nordic-Aryan Atlantis.

Monumental statue of Arminius/Hermann in the Teutoberg Forest.

Not to be outdone, in 1936 Himmler brought an archaeological research group into his ss structure as part of his fascination with Germanic heritage. This larger group became a section of the ss-Ahnenerbe (ancestral heritage), an umbrella organization that included many different historical disciplines to create a vision of the German past. The ss-Ahnenerbe did not confine its activities to the German heartland in central Europe. In addition to domestic research, it launched expeditions to seek evidence for Aryan precursors in the Near East and Tibet. An expedition to Bolivia was cancelled when the Second World War broke out. If this sounds familiar, it is because the ss-Ahnenerbe's overseas activities inspired the Nazi characters in the films *Raiders of the Lost Ark* (1981) and *Indiana Jones and the Last Crusade* (1989).

When Germany overran other parts of Europe, ss-Ahnenerbe archaeologists moved into occupied territories. In 1940–42, an ss-Ahnenerbe team conducted excavations at Biskupin, which they renamed Urstadt. After the fall of France in 1940, the Rosenberg group quickly moved in to investigate the menhirs at Carnac to see if they could make an Aryan connection, as part of a failed scheme to generate separatist sentiment in the Breton population. The ss-Ahnenerbe was not pleased that the Rosenberg organization had got there first, but the following year it redirected its attention to Crimea and the Caucasus.

After the war, some Nazi archaeologists were removed from the discipline or relegated to provincial assignments. Reinerth, for example, became director of the pile-dwelling museum in Unteruhldingen. Others, including Herbert Jankuhn (1905–1990), who became head of ss-Ahnenerbe's archaeology section in 1940, passed through a perfunctory de-Nazification process and went on to prominent academic careers.[12]

Meanwhile, back at Gergovia, the monumentalized site was put to use by Marshal Philippe Pétain (1856–1951) to legitimate his Vichy regime. In 1942, Pétain organized a commemoration around the monument erected in 1900, involving veterans of the First World War, to evoke the memory of Vercingetorix the hero and to link the Gaul to himself. Alésia had too much anti-German baggage, which would not have sat well with Vichy's overlords, so

Gergovia was a more palatable choice. No one was particularly impressed by this attempt to link the heroic Vercingetorix to the subservient Pétain.[13]

After the Second World War, archaeologists became much more aware of the potential of their field for political manipulation. They were chastened by the willingness of many of their colleagues to take up such activity in return for being allowed to practise their profession. Moreover, the discipline had moved away from methods employed by Kossinna to trace the presence of ethnic boundaries in later prehistory. Politicians are always there, however. For example, in the 1980s, François Mitterrand (1916–1996) had a monument erected at Bibracte and a decade later built a large museum there in an effort to link the Vercingetorix story to a pan-European 'Celtic' identity.[14] He even expressed a wish to be buried there, although that did not happen.

Heritage management

Today, the archaeological record of the Barbarian World is the province of an activity known as 'heritage management'. In a sense, heritage management channels the use of national patrimony into more benign paths, although still within a framework of stewardship for the material remains of the past. Participation by archaeologists is central to heritage management, and it now forms a major part of the programme at many international archaeological conferences. National heritage management programmes have resulted in excavation and preservation of many sites threatened by development as well as suppression of trade in illicit antiquities.

Each European country has a governmental agency charged with overseeing the archaeology of heritage management. Some of these agencies have a long historical legacy themselves. For example, the Swedish National Heritage Board (Riksantikvarieämbetet) can trace its lineage back to the seventeenth century. Often, these governmental agencies include representatives from archaeology, architecture, museums, planning, tourism and engineering, along with legal staff. In Scotland, the agency formerly known as Historic

Scotland was renamed Historic Environment Scotland in 2015 to reflect a more holistic view of heritage management.

Many of the countries whose territory constituted the Barbarian World are members of the European Union. The EU has an array of legislation to protect antiquities and also to suppress international trade in antiquities. While much of this trade comes from the Mediterranean and the Near East, artefacts of the Barbarian World are also in high demand by collectors who do not comprehend that their quest for these objects drives looting and destruction of sites. Let me appeal to the reader never to purchase antiquities from anyone. The archaeological record is our legacy from the past and should be available for all to experience in museums and through its professional study.

Infrastructure development throughout Europe, particularly in countries like Ireland and Poland that did not see much investment in roads and pipelines until recently, has driven an explosion in rescue archaeology. Rescue archaeology has been practised since the beginning of the field, but often in connection with local construction. Now motorways and pipelines are carving long slices across the countryside, and they often cut through areas rich in archaeological sites. In my own research in Poland, the building of the A-1 motorway has yielded an avalanche of new data on early farmers, as well as later prehistoric periods. The costs of such research are usually built into the contracts for the construction, leading to the use of the term 'developer-funded archaeology'. In addition to research institutions like universities and museums, private archaeology firms have been established by archaeologists to bid on rescue projects.

Please do not try exploring the Barbarian World yourself with a spade. Freelance excavation is illegal in just about every European country. Permits for archaeological investigation are issued by the authorities to accountable organizations. If you require contact with artefacts in the soil, you should find an archaeological project that accepts volunteers. The reader of this book will appreciate that ancient objects are only informative when the context of the find is recorded. Digging in the style of nineteenth-century antiquarians destroys key archaeological evidence.

Yet hardly a month passes without a new discovery of barbarian treasure by non-archaeologists being reported in the press. Many are the result of accidental finds during construction, which normally results in work being halted until archaeologists can investigate. The accidental discovery of objects and sites goes back to the very beginning of archaeology, and we have seen repeatedly how important discoveries have been made in this fashion. Often, such as in the case of the Dover Boat, important finds can be studied in the field and removed quickly for conservation. At other times, they trigger multi-year investigations.

At several points in this book, the discovery of sites by hobbyists using metal detectors has been mentioned. This might seem to contradict the statement above about the general illegality of freelance excavation. Laws about using metal detectors vary widely from country to country. In some countries, such as Luxembourg, unauthorized searching is illegal. Elsewhere, the laws are somewhat vague, in that they prohibit unauthorized searching specifically for archaeological finds or at known archaeological sites, but searching for modern coins and jewellery is considered to be acceptable. The trouble is that the metal detector cannot differentiate between a coin from 1990 and a bronze torc. This legal grey area means that metal detecting is a widespread hobby in much of Europe.

Unlike in the United States where metal detector users are reviled by professional archaeologists, a positive working relationship has emerged in some European countries between the archaeological community and metal-detectorists. Sites such as Uppåkra in Sweden have been mentioned in previous chapters as places in which this relationship has yielded good results. In Britain, it is recognized that objects might be found during activities such as gardening or walking as well as by metal detecting. The 1997 Portable Antiquities Scheme provides a way for gardeners (and metal detector users) to bring finds to the attention of the authorities and enable them to be documented.[15] Finders of treasure, defined as objects (excluding isolated unmodified coins) of which any part is gold or silver more than 300 years old, may receive a reward. Archaeologists are not eligible to collect.

Visiting the Barbarians

The most direct way of connecting with the Barbarian World is through the artefacts made by its inhabitants, the sites where they lived and buried their dead and, in some cases, the remains of the people themselves. Europe is full of archaeological museums as well as preserved and reconstructed sites. A complete guide to the museums and sites of the Barbarian World is beyond the scope of this book, but they can be found listed in every guidebook. Detailed national maps, particularly Ordnance Survey maps of the British Isles, often show site locations. Archaeological sites and museums are major tourist attractions, and reconstructions of prehistoric settlements are promoted by local authorities to encourage the growth of tourist services like restaurants and lodging.

Given the pride of these countries in their archaeological heritage, it is no surprise that many national museums have extensive displays of prehistoric objects excavated from the settlements,

Reconstructed Iron Age buildings, with mud-brick wall behind them, at the Heuneburg. Note the four-post granary between the two buildings on the right.

burials and bogs of their countries. You can start with major national museums, such as the National Museum of Ireland, the British Museum, the National Museum of Denmark, the Musée d'Archéologie Nationale in France and the State Museum of Antiquities in the Netherlands, but every large town across temperate Europe will have an archaeological museum. Archaeological exhibits are often combined with displays about natural history, such as the Lower Saxony Landesmuseum in Hannover or the Natural History Museum in Vienna. Elsewhere, museums are specifically devoted to regional archaeology, such as the Museum of Archaeology in Kraków, Poland, or local archaeology, like the Museum Hallstatt in Hallstatt, Austria.

In the countryside, many archaeological sites and open-air museums are open to visitors. Some sites, like Loughcrew in Ireland, are unattended, and the visitor can simply wander among the passage graves. Hillforts and *oppida* are usually open for walking around, and ship settings, like the one at Anundshög in Sweden, are right by the side of the road. Others, such as Stonehenge, offer the visitor a structured experience with more interpretive guidance, but usually with an admission charge.

In some cases, replicas of prehistoric structures have been built on top of the ancient site, such as at Biskupin in Poland or the Heuneburg in Germany. This practice is now frowned upon in heritage management since it can potentially damage the original remains. Elsewhere, archaeological sites have been reconstructed adjacent to the original sites, or in different locations altogether. Often this is in the name of 'experimental archaeology', the reconstruction of ancient things and structures to see how much work they entail, whether or not they stand up, and how they wear over time. Well-known examples of reconstructed ancient villages are Butser Farm in England and Lejre in Denmark. Often re-enactors inhabit these sites and attempt to live as barbarians. Biskupin hosts an annual Archaeological Festival at which visitors can experience ancient cuisine and watch demonstrations of barbarian activities.

Finally, a direct connection with the Barbarian World can be made by spending a moment with one of the people who inhabited it. Tollund Man resides in a display case in the Silkeborg Museum in central Jutland, while Grauballe Man is nearby in Aarhus. Lindow Man's body can be seen in the British Museum, and the National Museum in Dublin has what remains of Oldcroghan Man and Clonycavan Man. The occupants of the Bronze Age oak coffin burials can be seen in the National Museum in Copenhagen. Perhaps the most famous prehistoric corpse is that of Ötzi, the Iceman, who is in the South Tyrol Museum of Archaeology in Bolzano, Italy. After roaming through well-done exhibits that show the objects found with Ötzi in the slush-filled gully, visitors file by a climate-controlled compartment in which he reposes. His contorted and shrivelled mummified corpse can be seen through a small window, his hollow eyes eerily gazing back at the viewer. Although it feels a bit like a wake, visiting Ötzi is an excellent opportunity to feel a connection with the most famous representative of the fourth millennium BC in the twenty-first century AD.

In fact, a visitor might want to try an Ötzi product. There is Ötzi bread made with primeval grains. Ötzi pizza periodically makes an appearance in pizza parlours in the Alps. You can purchase the records of DJ Ötzi (stage name of Gerhard Fridle), an Austrian entertainer from the Tyrol. Perhaps the most memorable product bearing the Iceman's image is Ötzi 'ice and fire liqueur', whose manufacturer, the Tirol Herbal Distillery, says that it is 'A tightrope walk from one highlight to the next! A mysteriously fruity fire liqueur with "ice crystals" – delicious and stimulating, invigorating the senses.' You can drink it either neat, with ice or in a cocktail. Since Ötzi liqueur is 100 proof (50 per cent alcohol), it can be set on fire for a dramatic effect.

The Barbarian World today

After attending a NATO summit on 5 September 2014, U.S. President Barack Obama made a detour to visit Stonehenge. *USA Today* reports that he said, 'How cool is this? It's spectacular. It's a special place.'[16] Despite his not having demonstrated a prior fascination with prehistoric Europe, Obama's trip to visit an iconic prehistoric monument demonstrates the hold that the Barbarian World exercises over the popular imagination. The challenge for those who study these societies is to situate them in their context as known from archaeology and texts so they can be appreciated for their immense contribution to the human story.

Archaeological evidence continually increases in volume and complexity. Always remember that it presents only a fragmentary view of past life, a jigsaw puzzle with most pieces missing and no picture on the box. Unlike history, in which a primary source discovered centuries ago does not change except in its interpretation and its relationship to newly found sources, an archaeological find from an uncertain context actually can decrease in significance as new objects are discovered using better methods. New analytical techniques can take old finds and give them new life. Who could have foreseen a century ago that the girl in the Egtved coffin would now be able to tell us her story of movement and nutrition?

Ötzi 'ice and fire liqueur' exemplifies how the Iceman excites the modern imagination.

New archaeological discoveries are continually made through-out the Barbarian World. The most sensational of these find their way into the press, often with the assistance of press releases from communications offices at universities, museums and government agencies. Many have been highlighted in this book, including the recent discoveries at Stonehenge, Must Farm, Lavau and Sandby Borg. Other discoveries in the field and in the lab are not sufficiently surprising or unusual to merit press coverage, but rather provide small glimpses of life in the Barbarian World which eventually add up to one or two additional pieces to the jigsaw puzzle.

Melting snow and ice patches in the mountains of Scandinavia have revealed hundreds of new prehistoric finds. These objects were left behind by hunters and trappers who pursued game animals that congregated on these patches, especially during the summer. In 2011, archaeologists found a crumpled-up piece of fabric on the edge of an ice patch at Lendbreen, southern Norway.[17] When unfolded, it turned out to be a tunic, which was revealed by radio-carbon dating to have been made between AD 230 and 390. Its wool had been carefully selected to include both long, coarse fibres and fine, delicate fibres. It was skilfully woven into a diamond-pattern twill especially suited to high-altitude cold-weather wear, the North Face jacket of its day. Diamond twills are known from waterlogged weapon deposits such as those at Illerup Ådal and are frequently encountered in preserved textiles from the Roman World. Was the person whose tunic was found at Lendbreen a warrior, perhaps someone who had returned from Roman service, rather than a simple mountain hunter?

The Lendbreen tunic might not look spectacular. Yet the amount of information that can be extracted from a simple discovery like this helps connect more dots that make up our understanding of the Barbarian World. More objects remain to be discovered under the fields and bogs of temperate Europe, in its mountain recesses and especially off its coasts. Not all the Iron Age princely burials have been found, nor has the last weapon deposit been excavated. Even new megalithic tombs are sometimes revealed as peat and turf are peeled away. In the laboratory, new techniques from ana-lytical chemistry and archaeogenetics will lead to fresh insights.

The tunic from approximately AD 300 as found in the ice patch at Lendbreen, Norway.

The archaeological record will become even more complex, and interpretations will surely change. Additional ways will be found to incorporate the Barbarian World into a usable past for modern societies, some for the good, and unfortunately others for unsavoury purposes. Barbarians live on in the modern world, not just in museums but in the imaginations of all who inhabit or visit their ancient lands.

Introduction

1 Archaeologists generally continue to use 'bc' and 'ad' as chronological markers, despite their obvious origins in Christian belief. Many authors now use 'bce' for 'Before the Christian Era' and 'ce' for Christian Era, or even 'Common Era' (common to whom?), in an effort towards religious neutrality. The use of the traditional bc and ad in this book is mainly for consistency with scholarly literature both past and present. The ending date of ad 500 for this book was chosen somewhat arbitrarily, roughly corresponding to the collapse of the Roman Empire in the West.

2 Let me explain. The reference is to the play within Mel Brooks's movie and musical *The Producers* (1968 and 2001), and Arminius was the German chief who defeated the Romans in the Teutoberg Forest in ad 9.

3 Sometimes given as 'history will be kind to me because I intend to write it,' although there is no indication that Churchill actually said that. The above anecdote is given in Clifton Fadiman, *The Little, Brown Book of Anecdotes* (Boston, ma, 1985), p. 122.

4 An outstanding account of the origins and impact of the Three-age System is provided by Peter Rowley-Conwy, *From Genesis to Prehistory: The Archaeological Three Age System and its Contested Reception in Denmark, Britain, and Ireland* (Oxford, 2007).

5 Grahame Clark, *Prehistoric Europe: The Economic Basis* (London, 1952), pp. 10–11.

6 The first use of 'luminous' to describe areas that stand out in the archaeological record is found in Gordon Barclay, 'Introduction: A Regional Agenda?', in *Defining a Regional Neolithic: The Evidence from Britain and Ireland*, ed. Kenneth Brophy and Gordon Barclay (Oxford, 2009), p. 4. I have expanded the concept to the rest of Europe and the remainder of later prehistory.

1 Hunters, Fishers, Farmers and Metalworkers

1 The story of the Amesbury Archer, his 'Companion' and the Boscombe Bowmen, from discovery through analysis, is contained in Andrew P. Fitzpatrick, *The Amesbury Archer and the Boscombe Bowmen: Bell Beaker Burials on Boscombe Down, Amesbury, Wiltshire* (Salisbury, 2011).

2 Recent innovations in the application of analytical chemistry have yielded important insights for archaeologists, as we will see several more times in this book. Isotopes are different forms of the same element depending on the number of neutrons in their nuclei. Isotopes of oxygen vary depending on weather patterns and moisture. Isotopes of strontium vary in their ratios in rocks of different ages and compositions. Soils formed from these rocks, water that flows through these soils, plants, that absorb the water, and eventually animals and people who eat the plants, absorb the strontium isotopes in the same ratios.

3 Archaeologists refer to the periods discussed in this chapter as the Mesolithic and the Neolithic. The Mesolithic refers to hunter-gatherers living in temperate Europe after the establishment of modern environmental conditions, while the Neolithic encompasses sedentary people who used domesticated plants and animals. Those terms are not used here, to avoid jargon.

4 Søren H. Andersen, *Tybrind Vig: Submerged Mesolithic Settlements in Denmark* (Aarhus, 2014), pp. 169–85.

5 Lars Larsson, 'The Skateholm Project: Late Mesolithic Coastal Settlement in Southern Sweden', in *Case Studies in European Prehistory*, ed. Peter Bogucki (Boca Raton, FL, 1993), pp. 31–62.

6 In domestication, selection means breeding plants and animals with desirable characteristics and eating the rest.

7 Although some details have changed in the last twenty years, an overview of the spread of farming in Europe can be found in Peter Bogucki, 'The Spread of Early Farming in Europe', *American Scientist*, 84 (May–June 1996), pp. 242–53, and with a more current academic treatment in Peter Bogucki, 'Hunters, Fishers and Farmers of Northern Europe, 9000–3000 BCE', in Colin and Paul Bahn, eds, *The Cambridge World Prehistory*, vol. III (Cambridge, 2014), pp. 1835–59.

8 Peter Bogucki, 'The Largest Buildings in the World 7,000 Years Ago', *Archaeology*, XLVIII/6 (1995), pp. 57–9.

9 Christian Meyer et al., 'The Massacre Mass Grave of Schöneck-Kilianstädten Reveals New Insights into Collective Violence in Early Neolithic Central Europe', *Proceedings of the National Academy of Sciences*, CXII/36 (2015), pp. 11217–22.

10 The story of the discovery and early interpretation of the Swiss Lake Dwellings can be found in Francesco Menotti, *Wetland Archaeology and Beyond: Theory and Practice* (Oxford, 2012), pp. 3–9.

11 Jörg Schibler, Stephanie Jacomet and Alice Choyke, 'Arbon-Bleiche 3', in *Ancient Europe, 8000 BC–AD 1000: An Encyclopedia of the Barbarian*

World, vol. I, ed. Peter Bogucki and Pam J. Crabtree (New York, 2004), pp. 395–7.

12 Wolfram Schier, 'Central and Eastern Europe', in *The Oxford Handbook of Neolithic Europe*, ed. Chris Fowler, Jan Harding and Daniela Hofmann (Oxford, 2015), pp. 108–11.

13 A recent authoritative volume on prehistoric copper mining in Europe is William O'Brien, *Prehistoric Copper Mining in Europe, 5500–500 BC* (Oxford, 2014).

14 Every year new information about the Iceman becomes available. A readable account of his discovery and the first generation of analyses is Brenda Fowler, *Iceman: Uncovering the Life and Times of a Prehistoric Man Found in an Alpine Glacier* (New York, 2000). Recent studies have focused on the Iceman's genome and various pathogens he carried. See, for example, Frank Maixner et al., 'The 5300-year-old *Helicobacter pylori* Genome of the Iceman', *Science*, CCCLI/6269 (2016), pp. 162–5, and V. Coia et al., 'Whole Mitochondrial DNA Sequencing in Alpine Populations and the Genetic History of the Neolithic Tyrolean Iceman', *Scientific Reports*, VI, 18932; DOI: 10.1038/srep18932 (2016).

15 Ötzi can be visited at the South Tyrol Museum of Archaeology in Bolzano, and the museum's website has an extensive presentation of his equipment and clothing: www.iceman.it.

16 Although the poor preservation of his stomach mucosa does not permit this to be determined with certainty. See Maixner et al., 'The 5300-year-old *Helicobacter pylori* Genome of the Iceman', p. 164.

17 Klaus Oeggl et al., 'The Reconstruction of the Last Itinerary of Ötzi, the Neolithic Iceman, by Pollen Analyses from Sequentially Sampled Gut Extracts', *Quaternary Science Reviews*, XXVI/7 (2007), pp. 853–61.

18 Patrizia Pernter et al., 'Radiologic Proof for the Iceman's Cause of Death (ca. 5300 BP)', *Journal of Archaeological Science*, XXXIV/11 (2007), pp. 1784–86.

19 An authoritative overview of the megalithic monuments of the Barbarian World is Magdalena S. Midgley, *The Megaliths of Northern Europe* (London, 2008); see also many other guides, such as Chris Scarre, *Exploring Prehistoric Europe* (New York, 1998).

20 Although the Boyne tombs are the most celebrated of these groups, I find Loughcrew to be the most interesting archaeologically, and Carrowmore has been the most thoroughly investigated in recent decades. Unfortunately, many of the graves at Carrowkeel were dug with poor methods over a century ago.

21 An excellent overview can be found in Geraldine Stout, *Newgrange and the Bend of the Boyne* (Cork, 2002); see also Geraldine Stout and Matthew Stout, *Newgrange* (Cork, 2008).

22 For a critical evaluation of the Newgrange reconstruction, see Gabriel Cooney, 'Newgrange: A View from the Platform', *Antiquity*, LXXX/309 (2006), pp. 697–708.

23 The Heritage Council (Ireland), 'Significant Unpublished Archaeological Excavations, 1930–1997, Section 5, Megalithic Tombs/Neolithic Burial Practices', http://heritagecouncil.ie, accessed 2 July 2016.

24 Including, of course, *National Lampoon's European Vacation* (dir. Amy Heckerling, 1985) and *This Is Spiñal Tap* (dir. Rob Reiner, 1984).

25 The 2015 discovery of a 'superhenge' at Durrington Walls is the latest chapter in the Stonehenge story. See Elizabeth Palermo, 'Super-henge Revealed: A New English Mystery is Uncovered', www.livescience.com, 8 September 2015, among other reports.

26 Mike Parker Pearson et al., 'Stonehenge', in *The Oxford Handbook of the European Bronze Age*, ed. Harry Fokkens and Anthony Harding (Oxford, 2013), p. 160.

27 The current archaeological application of the word 'henge' has a specific meaning of an enclosure in which the bank is outside the ditch, so the early phase of Stonehenge technically is not a henge, but it is grandfathered into that category.

28 Parker Pearson, 'Stonehenge', p. 165.

29 Maria Dasi Espuig, 'Stonehenge Secrets Revealed by Underground Map', www.bbc.com/news, 10 September 2014.

30 Oliver E. Craig et al., 'Feeding Stonehenge: Cuisine and Consumption at the Late Neolithic Site of Durrington Walls', *Antiquity*, LXXXIX/347 (2015), pp. 1096–1109.

31 Vince Gaffney's interpretation is discussed by Ed Caesar in 'What Lies Beneath Stonehenge?' www.smithsonianmag.com, September 2014.

32 Gerald S. Hawkins, *Stonehenge Decoded* (Garden City, NY, 1965).

33 Clive L. N. Ruggles, 'Stonehenge and its Landscape', in *Handbook of Archaeoastronomy and Ethnoastronomy*, ed. Clive L. N. Ruggles (New York, 2015), pp. 1223–38.

2 Connections, Rituals and Symbols

1 William O'Brien, *Prehistoric Copper Mining in Europe, 5500–500 BC* (Oxford, 2014), pp. 105–7.

2 Stephen Shennan, 'Cost, Benefit and Value in the Organization of Early European Copper Production', *Antiquity*, LXXIII/280 (1999), pp. 356–7.

3 See www.nationalbanken.dk/en/banknotes_and_coins, accessed 15 September 2016.

4 Emília Pásztor, 'Nebra Disk', in *Handbook of Archaeoastronomy and Ethnoastronomy*, ed. Clive L. N. Ruggles (New York, 2015), pp. 1349–56.

5 Anthony F. Harding, *European Societies in the Bronze Age* (Cambridge, 2000), pp. 45–8.

6 Peter S. Wells, 'Investigating the Origins of Temperate Europe's First Towns: Excavations at Hascherkeller, 1978–1981', in *Case Studies in European Prehistory*, ed. Peter Bogucki (Boca Raton, FL, 1993), pp. 181–203.

7 Jason Urbanus, 'Fire in the Fens', *Archaeology*, LXX/1, pp. 34–9.
8 Robert Van de Noort, 'Seafaring and Riverine Navigation in the Bronze Age of Europe', in *The Oxford Handbook of the European Bronze Age*, ed. A. F. Harding and H. Fokkens (Oxford, 2013), pp. 382–97.
9 Ole Crumlin-Pedersen, 'The Dover Boat: A Reconstruction Case-study', *International Journal of Nautical Archaeology*, XXXV/1 (2006), pp. 58–71.
10 Johan Ling, 'War Canoes or Social Units? Human Representation in Rock-art Ships', *European Journal of Archaeology*, XV/3 (2012), pp. 465–85.
11 Stuart Needham, Andrew J. Lawson and Ann Woodward, '"A Noble Group of Barrows": Bush Barrow and the Normanton Down Early Bronze Age Cemetery Two Centuries On', *Antiquaries Journal*, XC (2010), pp. 1–39.
12 Bronze Age coffins, their occupants and their grave goods can be seen in the National Museum in Copenhagen: www.natmus.dk.
13 Karin Margarita Frei et al., 'Tracing the Dynamic Life Story of a Bronze Age Female', *Scientific Reports*, V, 10431; DOI: 10.1038/srep10431 (2015).
14 Mark Brennand et al., 'The Survey and Excavation of a Bronze Age Timber Circle at Holme-next-the-Sea, Norfolk, 1998–9', *Proceedings of the Prehistoric Society*, LXIX (2003), pp. 1–84.
15 Francis Pryor, *Flag Fen: Life and Death of a Prehistoric Landscape* (Stroud, 2005).
16 Joakim Goldhahn and Johan Ling, 'Bronze Age Rock Art in Northern Europe: Contexts and Interpretations', in *The Oxford Handbook of the European Bronze Age*, ed. A. F. Harding and H. Fokkens (Oxford, 2013), pp. 270–90. See also Ling, 'War Canoes or Social Units?'
17 Joakim Goldhahn, 'Bredarör on Kivik: A Monumental Cairn and the History of its Interpretation', *Antiquity*, LXXXIII/320 (2009), pp. 359–71.
18 See www.museum.ie/Archaeology, accessed 1 December 2016, particularly the exhibit 'Ór – Ireland's Gold', both on display at the museum and on their website.
19 Mary Cahill, 'Irish Bronze Age Goldwork', in *Ancient Europe, 8000 BC–AD 1000: Encyclopedia of the Barbarian World*, vol. II, ed. Peter Bogucki and Pam J. Crabtree (New York, 2004), pp. 69–71.
20 Christopher D. Standish et al., 'A Non-local Source of Irish Chalcolithic and Early Bronze Age Gold', *Proceedings of the Prehistoric Society*, LXXXI (2015), pp. 149–77.
21 Dermot F. Gleeson, 'Discovery of Gold Gorget at Burren, Co. Clare', *Journal of the Royal Society of Antiquaries of Ireland*, IV/1 (1934), pp. 138–9.

3 TRADE, SALT, GREEKS AND WEALTH

1 Michael N. Geselowitz, 'Technology and Social Change: Ironworking in the Rise of Social Complexity in Iron Age Central Europe', in *Tribe and Polity in Late Prehistoric Europe*, ed. D. Blair Gibson and Michael N. Geselowitz (New York, 1988), pp. 137–54.
2 Among many, Barry W. Cunliffe, *The Ancient Celts* (Oxford, 1997) remains the best. Michael Morse's *How the Celts Came to Britain* (Stroud, 2005)

investigates the social and cultural construction of 'Celtic' in scholarship beginning in the eighteenth century and continuing today.

3 Józef Kostrzewski, 'Biskupin: An Early Iron Age Village in Western Poland', *Antiquity*, XII/47 (1938), pp. 311–17. See also Anthony Harding and Włodzimierz Rączkowski, 'Living on the Lake in the Iron Age: New Results from Aerial Photographs, Geophysical Survey and Dendrochronology on Sites of Biskupin Type', *Antiquity*, LXXXIV/324 (2010), pp. 386–404.

4 Wojciech Piotrowski, 'The Importance of the Biskupin Wet Site for Twentieth-century Polish Archaeology', in *Hidden Dimensions: The Cultural Significance of Wetland Archaeology*, ed. Kathryn Bernick (Vancouver, 1998), pp. 90–98.

5 Ibid., p. 98.

6 Harding and Rączkowski, 'Living on the Lake in the Iron Age', pp. 389–98.

7 Anton Kern et al., *Kingdom of Salt: 7000 Years of Hallstatt* (Vienna, 2009). For a broader context of Hallstatt and salt production in prehistoric Europe, see Anthony Harding, *Salt in Prehistoric Europe* (Leiden, 2013).

8 These, and many other objects preserved in the salt and from the nearby cemetery, can be seen at the Natural History Museum in Vienna: www.nhm-wien.ac.at/en.

9 Bruno Chaume and Claude Mordant, *Le Complexe aristocratique de Vix: Nouvelles recherches sur l'habitat et le système de fortification et l'environnement du Mont Lassois* (Dijon, 2011).

10 Bettina Arnold, 'Eventful Archaeology, the Heuneburg Mudbrick Wall, and the Early Iron Age of Southwest Germany', in *Eventful Archaeologies: New Approaches to Social Transformation in the Archaeological Record*, ed. Douglas J. Bolender (Albany, NY, 2010), pp. 100–114.

11 Manuel Fernández-Götz and Dirk Krausse, 'Rethinking Early Iron Age Urbanisation in Central Europe: The Heuneburg Site and its Archaeological Environment', *Antiquity*, LXXXVII/336 (June 2013), pp. 473–87.

12 Bettina Arnold, 'A Landscape of Ancestors: The Space and Place of Death in Iron Age West-central Europe', in *The Space and Place of Death*, ed. Helaine Silverman and David B. Small (Washington, DC, 2002), pp. 129–43.

13 Jörg Biel, 'The Late Hallstatt Chieftain's Grave at Hochdorf', *Antiquity*, LV/213 (1981), pp. 16–18. The Keltenmuseum Hochdorf displays the finds from the tomb; see www.keltenmuseum.de.

14 J.V.S. Megaw, 'The Vix Burial', *Antiquity*, XL/157 (1966), pp. 38–44

15 Jason Urbanus, 'Eternal Banquets of the Early Celts', *Archaeology*, LXVIII/6 (November–December 2015), pp. 44–9; see also 'Une tombe princière celte du Vᵉ siècle avant notre ère découverte à Lavau', www.inrap.fr, 10 March 2015/18 July 2016.

16 Niall M. Sharples, *English Heritage Book of Maiden Castle* (London, 1991).

17 Barry W. Cunliffe, 'Danebury: The Anatomy of a Hillfort Re-exposed', in *Case Studies in European Prehistory*, ed. Peter Bogucki (Boca Raton, FL, 1993), pp. 259–86.

4 Romans Encounter the High Iron Age

1 This is not a term used by archaeologists, simply an expression invented for this book to characterize barbarian social, technological and artistic complexity encountered by the Romans and seen in archaeological data.

2 Mette Løvschal and Mads Kähler Holst, 'Repeating Boundaries – Repertoires of Landscape Regulations in Southern Scandinavia in the Late Bronze Age and Pre-Roman Iron Age', *Danish Journal of Archaeology*, iii/2 (2014), pp. 95–118.

3 Fokke Gerritsen, 'Domestic Times: Houses and Temporalities in Late Prehistoric Europe', in *Prehistoric Europe: Theory and Practice*, ed. Andrew Jones (Oxford, 2008), pp. 143–61.

4 Stijn Arnoldussen and Richard Jansen, 'Iron Age Habitation Patterns on the Southern and Northern Dutch Pleistocene Coversand Soils: The Process of Settlement Nucleation', in *Haus-Gehöft-Weiler-Dorf. Siedlungen der vorrömischen Eisenzeit im nördlichen Mitteleuropa*, ed. M. Meyer (Rahden/Westfalen, 2010), pp. 379–97.

5 Arthur Bulleid and Harold St George Gray, *The Glastonbury Lake Village: A Full Description of the Excavations and the Relics Discovered, 1892–1907* (Glastonbury, 1911); see also Stephen Minnitt, 'The Iron Age Wetlands of Central Somerset', in *Somerset Archaeology: Papers to Mark 150 Years of the Somerset Archaeological and Natural History Society*, ed. C. J. Webster (Taunton, 2001), pp. 73–8.

6 Gerard Aalbersberg and Tony Brown, 'The Environment and Context of the Glastonbury Lake Village: A Re-assessment', *Journal of Wetland Archaeology*, x/1 (2013), pp. 136–51.

7 See Carole L. Crumley, 'Heterarchy and the Analysis of Complex Societies', in *Heterarchy and the Analysis of Complex Societies*, ed. Robert Ehrenreich, Carole L. Crumley and Janet Levy (Washington, dc, 1995), pp. 1–5, for a seminal discussion.

8 Richard Brunning and Conor McDermott, 'Trackways and Roads across the Wetlands', in *The Oxford Handbook of Wetland Archaeology*, ed. Francesco Menotti (Oxford, 2012), pp. 359–84, provides a comprehensive overview.

9 Barry Raftery, 'Ancient Trackways in Corlea Bog, Co. Longford', *Archaeology Ireland*, 1/2 (1987), pp. 60–64; Brunning and McDermott, 'Trackways and Roads across the Wetlands', p. 365. The Corlea trackway has been preserved and has a visitor centre.

10 See Miranda J. Aldhouse-Green, *Bog Bodies Uncovered: Solving Europe's Ancient Mystery* (London, 2015), for a comprehensive overview, while Wijnand A. B. van der Sanden, 'Bog Bodies: Underwater Burials, Sacrifices and Executions', in *The Oxford Handbook of Wetland Archaeology*, ed. Francesco Menotti (Oxford, 2013), pp. 401–16, is a more compact review.

11 Tollund Man is in the Silkeborg Museum and can be seen in detailed photos on their website: www.tollundman.dk.

12 Karen E. Lange, 'Tales from the Bog', *National Geographic Magazine*, http://ngm.nationalgeographic.com, September 2007.
13 Where he can be visited today: see www.moesgaardmuseum.dk/en.
14 Lindow Man can be seen on display at the British Museum in London: see www.britishmuseum.org.
15 Eamonn P. Kelly, 'An Archaeological Interpretation of Irish Iron Age Bog Bodies', in *The Archaeology of Violence: Interdisciplinary Approaches*, ed. Sarah Ralph (Albany, NY, 2013), pp. 232–40. See also Lange, 'Tales from the Bog'. Clonycavan and Oldcroghan Men can be visited in the National Museum, Dublin: see www.museum.ie/Archaeology.
16 Kelly, 'An Archaeological Interpretation of Irish Iron Age Bog Bodies', p. 239.
17 Jørgen Jensen, 'The Hjortspring Boat Reconstructed', *Antiquity*, LXIII/240 (1989), pp. 531–5.
18 Klavs Randsborg, *Hjortspring: Warfare and Sacrifice in Early Europe* (Aarhus, 1995), pp. 38–42; see also Flemming Kaul, 'The Hjortspring Find: The Oldest of the Large Nordic War Booty Sacrifices', in *The Spoils of Victory: The North in the Shadow of the Roman Empire*, ed. Lars Jørgensen, Birger Storgaard and Lone Gebauer Thomsen (Copenhagen, 2003), p. 218.
19 Barry W. Cunliffe, *Hengistbury Head: The Prehistoric and Roman Settlement, 3500 BC–AD 500*, vol. I (Oxford, 1987).
20 Barry W. Cunliffe, 'Britain and the Continent: Networks of Interaction', in *A Companion to Roman Britain*, ed. Malcolm Todd (Oxford, 2003), pp. 1–11.
21 Nico Roymans, *Ethnic Identity and Imperial Power: The Batavians in the Early Roman Empire* (Amsterdam, 2004), p. 4.
22 Colin Wells, 'What's New Along the Lippe: Recent Work in North Germany', *Britannia*, XXIX (1998), pp. 457–64.
23 S. Von Schnurbein, 'Augustus in Germania and His New "Town" at Waldgirmes East of the Rhine', *Journal of Roman Archaeology*, XVI (2003), pp. 93–107.
24 See Tony Clunn, *Quest for the Lost Roman Legions: Discovering the Varus Battlefield* (El Dorado Hills, CA, 2009).
25 Peter S. Wells, *The Battle That Stopped Rome: Emperor Augustus, Arminius, and the Slaughter of the Legions in the Teutoburg Forest* (New York, 2003).
26 The recent find of a slaughtered army in the Alken Enge bog in Jutland, Denmark, suggests that perhaps leaving skeletons of the defeated on the battlefield was a more widespread practice. See Irene Berg Petersen, 'An Entire Army Sacrificed in a Bog', http://sciencenordic.com, 22 August 2012.
27 Strontium isotope analysis indicates that four of the individuals came from either Bavaria or Bohemia, which has been interpreted as representing remains of Germanic warriors disposed of after a failed attack. See Josef Mühlenbrock and Mike Schweissing, '"Frisch Erforscht!": Die Skelette aus dem römischen Töpferofen in Haltern am See', *Archäologie in Westfalen-Lippe 2009* (2010), pp. 261–5.
28 Gabi Rasbach, 'Waldgirmes', *Archaeological Journal*, CLXX, supp. 1 (2013), pp. 18–21.

29 Maria Jażdżewska, 'A Roman Legionary Helmet Found in Poland', *Gladius*, XVII (1986), pp. 57–62.

30 Michael Meyer, 'Roman Cultural Influence in Western Germania Magna', in *The Oxford Handbook of the Archaeology of Roman Germany*, ed. Simon James and Stefan Krmnicek (Oxford, 2015), DOI: 10.1093/oxfordhb/9780199665730.013.8 (accessed 9 July 2016).

31 Timothy Taylor, 'The Gundestrup Cauldron', *Scientific American*, CCLXI (1992), pp. 84–9. The Gundestrup Cauldron can be seen at the National Museum in Copenhagen, and there is a detailed presentation of the cauldron on the museum's website: http://en.natmus.dk/historical-knowledge/denmark/prehistoric-period-until-1050-ad/the-early-iron-age/the-gundestrup-cauldron, accessed 15 September 2016.

5 Barbarians beyond the Imperial Frontier

1 William O'Brien, *Iverni: A Prehistory of Cork* (Cork, 2012), p. 3.

2 In the historical literature, the term *limes* is often used to refer to the boundaries of Imperial Rome. It seems, however, that this term was not used by the Romans themselves while the boundary was maintained, but rather seems to have come into use later.

3 Peter A. Wells, *The Barbarians Speak* (Princeton, NJ, 1999), p. 94.

4 Guy Halsall, 'Two Worlds Become One: A "Counter-intuitive" View of the Roman Empire and "Germanic" Migration', *Germanic History*, XXXII (2014), p. 525.

5 To paraphrase the remark by Winston Churchill in a radio address on 20 January 1940.

6 Alexander Bursche, 'Contacts between the Late Roman Empire and North-central Europe', *Antiquaries Journal*, LXXVI/1 (1996), p. 34.

7 Kai Ruffing, 'Friedliche Beziehungen. Der Handel zwischen den römischen Provinzen und Germanien', in *Feindliche Nachbarn: Rom und die Germanen*, ed. Helmuth Schneider (Cologne, 2008), p. 162.

8 Summarized in Susan A. Johnston, 'Revisiting the Royal Sites', *Emania*, XX (2006), pp. 53–9.

9 Susan A. Johnston, Pam J. Crabtree and Douglas V. Campana, 'Performance, Place and Power at Dún Ailinne, a Ceremonial Site of the Irish Iron Age', *World Archaeology*, XLVI/2 (2014), pp. 206–23.

10 Bursche, 'Contacts between the Late Roman Empire and North-central Europe', p. 34.

11 Halsall, 'Two Worlds Become One', p. 525.

12 Kenneth Harl, *Coinage in the Roman Economy* (Baltimore, MD, 1996), p. 296.

13 Svante Fischer, Fernando López-Sánchez and Helena Victor, 'The 5th Century Hoard of Theodosian Solidi from Stora Brunneby, Öland, Sweden: A Result from the Leo Project', *Fornvännen*, CVI/3 (2011), p. 189.

14 Svante Fischer, *Roman Imperialism and Runic Literacy: The Westernization of Northern Europe (150–800 AD)*, series AUN 33 (Uppsala, 2005).

15 Artur Błażejewski, 'The Amber Road in Poland: State of Research and
    Perspectives', *Archaeologia Lituana*, XII (2015), pp. 57–63.

16 Leonardo Gregoratti, 'North Italic Settlers along the "Amber Route"',
    Studia Antiqua et Archaeologica, XIX/1 (2013), p. 141.

17 Charlotte Fabech and Ulf Näsman, 'Ritual Landscapes and Sacral Places
    in the First Millennium AD in South Scandinavia', in *Sacred Sites and Holy
    Places: Exploring the Sacralization of Landscape through Time and Space*,
    ed. S. W. Nordeide and S. Brink (Turnhout, 2013), pp. 53–109.

18 T. Douglas Price, *Ancient Scandinavia: An Archaeological History from the
    First Humans to the Vikings* (New York, 2015), p. 317.

19 Klavs Randsborg, 'Beyond the Roman Empire: Archaeological Discoveries
    in Gudme on Funen, Denmark', *Oxford Journal of Archaeology*, IX/3
    (1990), pp. 355–66; see also papers in Poul Otto Nielsen, Klavs Randsborg
    and Henrik Thrane, eds, *The Archaeology of Gudme and Lundeborg:
    Papers Presented at a Conference at Svendborg, October 1991*
    (Copenhagen, 1994).

20 Andres S. Dobat, 'Between Rescue and Research: An Evaluation after 30
    Years of Liberal Metal Detecting in Archaeological Research and Heritage
    Practice in Denmark', *European Journal of Archaeology*, XVI/4 (2013),
    pp. 704–25.

21 L. Jørgensen, 'Gudme-Lundeborg on Funen as a Model for Northern
    Europe?', in *The Gudme/Gudhem Phenomenon*, ed. O. Grimm and
    A. Pesch (Neumünster, 2011), pp. 77–89.

22 The story of the excavations at Uppåkra can be found at
    http://uppakra.se/en, accessed 1 December 2016.

23 Mikael Larsson and Dominic Ingemark, 'Roman Horticulture Beyond the
    Frontier: Garden Cultivation at Iron Age Uppåkra (Sweden)', *Journal of
    Roman Archaeology*, XXVIII (2015), pp. 393–402.

24 Lars Larsson, 'The Iron Age Ritual Building at Uppåkra, Southern Sweden',
    Antiquity, LXXXI/311 (2007), pp. 11–25.

25 Among many publications on the Nydam boats dating back to the
    nineteenth century, a good overview is Flemming Rieck, 'The Ships
    from Nydam Bog', in *The Spoils of Victory: The North in the Shadow
    of the Roman Empire*, ed. L. Jørgensen, B. Storgaard and L. G. Thomsen
    (Copenhagen 2003), pp. 296–309.

26 Unfortunately, the pine boat was cut up for firewood: Price, *Ancient
    Scandinavia*, p. 296.

27 Jørgen Ilkjær, *Illerup Ådal – Archaeology as a Magic Mirror* (Højbjerg-
    Moesgard, 2000); see also Price, *Ancient Scandinavia*, pp. 295–6.

28 Andres S. Dobat et al., 'The Four Horses of an Iron Age Apocalypse:
    War-horses from the Third-century Weapon Sacrifice at Illerup Aadal
    (Denmark)', *Antiquity*, LXXXVIII/339 (2014), pp. 191–204.

29 Halsall, 'Two Worlds Become One', p. 516.

30 Peter J. Heather, *Empires and Barbarians: The Fall of Rome and the Birth of
    Europe* (New York, 2010), pp. 28–35.

31 Halsall, 'Two Worlds Become One', p. 528.

32 An expression used by American archaeologist David Anthony (1990) to argue for the continued validity of migration as a mechanism of cultural change; see David W. Anthony, 'Migration in Archeology: The Baby and the Bathwater', *American Anthropologist*, xcii/4 (1990), pp. 895–914.

33 A complete discussion of the Goths will be found in the companion volume in this series, *The Goths: Lost Civilizations* (London, forthcoming).

34 Laurie Reitsema and Tomasz Kozłowski, 'Diet and Society in Poland before the State: Stable Isotope Evidence from a Wielbark Population (2nd c. AD)', *Anthropological Review*, lxxvi/1 (2013), pp. 1–22.

35 Przemysław Urbańczyk, 'The Goths in Poland: Where Did They Come From and When Did They Leave?', *European Journal of Archaeology*, i/3 (1998), pp. 397–415.

36 Ibid., p. 404.

37 Michael Kulikowski, *Rome's Gothic Wars: From the Third Century to Alaric* (New York, 2007), pp. 49–56.

38 Walter Goffart, *The Narrators of Barbarian History (AD 550–800): Jordanes, Gregory of Tours, Bede, and Paul the Deacon* (Princeton, NJ, 1988), pp. 105–11.

39 Heather, *Empires and Barbarians*, pp. 123–34.

40 László Bartosiewicz, 'Huns', in *Ancient Europe, 8000 BC–1000 AD: An Encyclopedia of the Barbarian World*, vol. ii, ed. Peter Bogucki and Pam J. Crabtree (New York, 2004), pp. 391–3.

41 Cameron Barnes, 'Rehorsing the Huns', *War and Society*, xxxiv/1 (2015), pp. 1–22.

42 An authoritative traditional account is Peter Hunter Blair, *An Introduction to Anglo-Saxon England*, 3rd edn (Cambridge, 2003).

43 In favour of settlement continuity, see Ken Dark, *Britain and the End of the Roman Empire* (Stroud, 2002), pp. 27–57; for separation between natives and migrants based on genetic studies, see Mark G. Stumpf, P. H. Michael and Heinrich Härke, 'Evidence for an Apartheid-like Social Structure in Early Anglo-Saxon England', *Proceedings of the Royal Society of London B: Biological Sciences*, cclxxiii/1601 (2006), pp. 2651–7.

44 Stanley West, *West Stow: The Anglo-Saxon Village, East Anglian Archaeology*, 24 (Ipswich, 1985).

45 Pam Crabtree, 'Sheep, Horses, Swine, and Kine: A Zooarchaeological Perspective on the Anglo-Saxon Settlement of England', *Journal of Field Archaeology*, xvi (1989), pp. 205–13.

46 Susan S. Hughes et al., 'Anglo-Saxon Origins Investigated by Isotopic Analysis of Burials from Berinsfield, Oxfordshire, UK', *Journal of Archaeological Science*, xlii (2014), pp. 81–92.

47 Bailey Young, 'Tomb of Childeric', in *Ancient Europe, 8000 BC–1000 AD: An Encyclopedia of the Barbarian World*, vol. ii, pp. 519–24.

48 Svante Fischer and Lennart Lind, 'The Coins in the Grave of King Childeric', *Journal of Archaeology and Ancient History*, xiv (2015), pp. 3–36.

49 Bonnie Effros, *Merovingian Mortuary Archaeology and the Making of the Early Middle Ages* (Berkeley, CA, 2003).

50 Andrew Curry, 'Öland, Sweden. Spring, AD 480', *Archaeology*, LXIX/2 (2016), pp. 26–31.

6 BARBARIANS LIVE ON

1 Henry Steele Commager, 'The Search for a Usable Past', in *The Search for a Usable Past and Other Essays in Historiography*, ed. Henry Steele Commager (New York, 1967), pp. 3–27.

2 René Goscinny, *René Goscinny raconte les secrets d'Astérix* (Paris, 2014). Carine Picaud, ed., *Astérix de A à Z* (Paris, 2013) is a collection of short discussions of the social context of Astérix ancient and modern that was prepared for an exhibition on Astérix at the National Library of France.

3 'Les Gaulois debunks Astérix', www.news24.com, 19 October 2011.

4 See www.alansorrell.ukartists.com.

5 Greg Bailey, 'Television and Archaeology: Views from the UK and Beyond', in *Encyclopedia of Global Archaeology*, ed. Claire Smith (New York, 2014), p. 7254.

6 Norman Hammond, 'Obituary: Glyn Edmund Daniel, 1914–1986', *American Antiquity*, LIV/2 (1989), pp. 234–9.

7 See www.newgrange.com/solstice-lottery.htm, accessed 15 September 2016.

8 Michael Dietler, 'A Tale of Three Sites: The Monumentalization of Celtic Oppida and the Politics of Collective Memory and Identity', *World Archaeology*, XXX/1 (1998), pp. 72–89.

9 Andreas Musolff, 'From Teamchef Arminius to Hermann Junior: Glocalised Discourses about a National Foundation Myth', *Language and Intercultural Communication*, XII/1 (2012), pp. 24–36.

10 Peter Bogucki, 'Ancient Europe: The Discovery of Antiquity', in *The History of Archaeology: An Introduction*, ed. Paul Bahn (London, 2014), pp. 27–8.

11 Bettina Arnold, 'The Past as Propaganda: How Hitler's Archaeologists Distorted European Prehistory to Justify Racist and Territorial Goals', *Archaeology*, 45 (July–August 1992), pp. 30–37, and Bettina Arnold, '"Arierdämmerung": Race and Archaeology in Nazi Germany', *World Archaeology*, XXXVIII/1 (2006), pp. 8–31.

12 Monika Steinel, 'Archaeology, National Socialism, and Rehabilitation: The Case of Herbert Jahnkuhn (1905–1990)', in *Ethics and the Archaeology of Violence*, ed. A. González-Ruibal and G. Moshenska (New York, 2015), pp. 153–65.

13 Dietler, 'A Tale of Three Sites', pp. 80–81.

14 Ibid., p. 82.

15 Portable Antiquities Scheme, www.finds.org.uk.

16 'Obama at Stonehenge: "How Cool is This?"', *USA Today*, www.usatoday.com, 5 September 2014.

17 Marianne Vedeler and Lise Bender Jørgensen, 'Out of the Norwegian Glaciers: Lendbreen – a Tunic from the Early First Millennium AD', *Antiquity*, LXXXVII/337 (2013), pp. 788–801.

Aalbersberg, Gerard, and Tony Brown, 'The Environment and Context of the Glastonbury Lake Village: A Re-assessment', *Journal of Wetland Archaeology*, x/1 (2013), pp. 136–51

Aldhouse-Green, Miranda J., *Bog Bodies Uncovered: Solving Europe's Ancient Mystery* (London, 2015)

Andersen, Søren H., *Ronæs Skov: Marinarkæologiske Undersøgelser Af En Kystboplads Fra Ertebølletid* (Højbjerg, 2009)

—, *Tybrind Vig: Submerged Mesolithic Settlements in Denmark* (Aarhus, 2014)

Anthony, David W., 'Migration in Archeology: The Baby and the Bathwater', *American Anthropologist*, xcii/4 (1990), pp. 895–914

Arnold, Bettina, '"Arierdämmerung": Race and Archaeology in Nazi Germany', *World Archaeology*, xxxviii/1 (2006), pp. 8–31

—, 'Eventful Archaeology, the Heuneburg Mudbrick Wall, and the Early Iron Age of Southwest Germany', in *Eventful Archaeologies: New Approaches to Social Transformation in the Archaeological Record*, ed. D. J. Bolender (Albany, NY, 2010), pp. 100–114

—, 'A Landscape of Ancestors: The Space and Place of Death in Iron Age West-central Europe', in *The Space and Place of Death*, ed. H. Silverman and D. B. Small (Washington, DC, 2002), pp. 129–43

—, 'The Past as Propaganda: How Hitler's Archaeologists Distorted European Prehistory to Justify Racist and Territorial Goals', *Archaeology* (July–August 1992), pp. 30–37

Arnoldussen, Stijn, and Richard Jansen, 'Iron Age Habitation Patterns on the Southern and Northern Dutch Pleistocene Coversand Soils: The Process of Settlement Nucleation', in *Haus-Gehöft-Weiler-Dorf. Siedlungen der vorrömischen Eisenzeit im nördlichen Mitteleuropa*, ed. M. Meyer (Rahden, 2010), pp. 379–97

Bailey, Greg, 'Television and Archaeology: Views from the UK and Beyond', in *Encyclopedia of Global Archaeology*, ed. C. Smith (New York, 2014), pp. 7253–9

Barclay, Gordon, 'Introduction: A Regional Agenda?', in *Defining a Regional Neolithic: The Evidence from Britain and Ireland*, ed. K. Brophy and G. Barclay (Oxford, 2009), pp. 1–4

Barnes, Cameron, 'Rehorsing the Huns', *War and Society*, XXXIV/1 (2015), pp. 1–22

Bartosiewicz, László, 'Huns', in *Ancient Europe, 8000 BC–AD 1000: An Encyclopedia of the Barbarian World*, ed. P. Bogucki and P. J. Crabtree, vol. II (New York, 2004), pp. 391–3

Biel, Jörg, 'The Late Hallstatt Chieftain's Grave at Hochdorf', *Antiquity*, LV/213 (1981), pp. 16–18

Blair, Peter Hunter, *An Introduction to Anglo-Saxon England*, 3rd edn (Cambridge, 2003)

Błażejewski, Artur, 'The Amber Road in Poland: State of Research and Perspectives', *Archaeologia Lituana*, XII (2015), pp. 57–63

Bogucki, Peter, 'Ancient Europe: The Discovery of Antiquity', in *The History of Archaeology: An Introduction*, ed. P. Bahn (London, 2014), pp. 15–38

——, 'Hunters, Fishers and Farmers of Northern Europe, 9000–3000 BCE', in *The Cambridge World Prehistory*, ed. C. Renfrew and P. Bahn, vol. III (Cambridge, 2014), pp. 1835–59

——, 'The Largest Buildings in the World 7,000 Years Ago', *Archaeology*, XLVIII/6 (1995), pp. 57–9

——, 'The Spread of Early Farming in Europe', *American Scientist*, 84 (May–June 1996), pp. 242–53

——, and Pam J. Crabtree, eds, *Ancient Europe, 8000 BC–AD 1000: An Encyclopedia of the Barbarian World*, 2 vols, (New York, 2004)

Brennand, Mark, et al., 'The Survey and Excavation of a Bronze Age Timber Circle at Holme-next-the-Sea, Norfolk, 1998–9', *Proceedings of the Prehistoric Society*, LXIX (2003), pp. 1–84

Brophy, Kenneth, and Gordon Barclay, eds, *Defining a Regional Neolithic: The Evidence from Britain and Ireland* (Oxford, 2009)

Brunning, Richard, and Conor McDermott, 'Trackways and Roads across the Wetlands', in *The Oxford Handbook of Wetland Archaeology*, ed. F. Menotti (Oxford, 2012), pp. 359–84

Bulleid, Arthur, and Harold St George Gray, *The Glastonbury Lake Village: A Full Description of the Excavations and the Relics Discovered, 1892–1907* (Glastonbury, 1911)

Bursche, Aleksander, 'Contacts between the Late Roman Empire and North-central Europe', *Antiquaries Journal*, LXXVI/1 (1996), pp. 31–50

Cahill, Mary, 'Irish Bronze Age Goldwork', *Ancient Europe, 8000 BC–AD 1000: An Encyclopedia of the Barbarian World*, ed. P. Bogucki and P. J. Crabtree, vol. II (New York, 2004), pp. 69–71

Chaume, Bruno, and Claude Mordant, *Le Complexe aristocratique de Vix: Nouvelles recherches sur l'habitat et le système de fortification et l'environnement du Mont Lassois* (Dijon, 2011)

Clark, Grahame, *Prehistoric Europe: The Economic Basis* (London, 1952)

Coia, V., et al., 'Whole Mitochondrial DNA Sequencing in Alpine Populations and the Genetic History of the Neolithic Tyrolean Iceman', *Scientific Reports*, VI, 18932; DOI: 10.1038/srep18932 (2016)

Commager, Henry Steele, 'The Search for a Usable Past', in *The Search for a Usable Past and Other Essays in Historiography*, ed. H. S. Commager (New York, 1967)

Cooney, Gabriel, 'Newgrange: A View from the Platform', *Antiquity*, LXXX/309 (2006), pp. 697–708

Crabtree, Pam J., 'Sheep, Horses, Swine, and Kine: A Zooarchaeological Perspective on the Anglo-Saxon Settlement of England', *Journal of Field Archaeology*, XVI/2 (1989), pp. 205–13

Craig, Oliver E., et al., 'Feeding Stonehenge: Cuisine and Consumption at the Late Neolithic Site of Durrington Walls', *Antiquity*, LXXXIX/347 (2015), pp. 1096–1109

Crumley, Carole L., 'Heterarchy and the Analysis of Complex Societies', in *Heterarchy and the Analysis of Complex Societies*, ed. R. Ehrenreich, C. L. Crumley and J. Levy (Washington, DC, 1995), pp. 1–5

Crumlin-Pedersen, Ole, 'The Dover Boat: A Reconstruction Case-Study', *International Journal of Nautical Archaeology*, XXXV/1 (2006), pp. 58–71

Cunliffe, Barry W., *The Ancient Celts* (Oxford, 1997)

——, 'Britain and the Continent: Networks of Interaction', in *A Companion to Roman Britain*, ed. M. Todd (Oxford, 2003), pp. 1–11

——, *Britain Begins* (Oxford, 2013)

——, 'Danebury, the Anatomy of a Hillfort Re-exposed', in *Case Studies in European Prehistory*, ed. P. Bogucki (Boca Raton, FL, 1993), pp. 259–86

——, *Hengistbury Head: The Prehistoric and Roman Settlement, 3500 BC–AD 500*, vol. I (Oxford, 1987)

Curry, Andrew, 'Öland, Sweden. Spring, AD 480', *Archaeology*, LXIX/2 (2016), pp. 26–31

Dark, Ken, *Britain and the End of the Roman Empire* (Stroud, 2002)

Dietler, Michael, 'A Tale of Three Sites: The Monumentalization of Celtic Oppida and the Politics of Collective Memory and Identity', *World Archaeology*, XXX/1 (1998), pp. 72–89

Dobat, Andres S., Between Rescue and Research: An Evaluation after 30 Years of Liberal Metal Detecting in Archaeological Research and Heritage Practice in Denmark', *European Journal of Archaeology*, XVI/4 (2013), pp. 704–25

——, et al., 'The Four Horses of an Iron Age Apocalypse: War-horses from the Third-century Weapon Sacrifice at Illerup Aadal (Denmark)', *Antiquity*, LXXXVIII/339 (2014), pp. 191–204

Fabech, Charlotte, and Ulf Näsman, 'Ritual Landscapes and Sacral Places in the First Millennium AD in South Scandinavia', in *Sacred Sites and Holy Places: Exploring the Sacralization of Landscape through Time and Space*, ed. S. W. Nordeide and S. Brink (Turnhout, 2013), pp. 53–110

Fernández-Götz, Manuel, and Dirk Krausse, 'Rethinking Early Iron Age Urbanisation in Central Europe: The Heuneburg Site and its Archaeological Environment', *Antiquity*, LXXXVII/336 (2013), pp. 473–87

Fischer, Svante, and Lennart Lind, 'The Coins in the Grave of King Childeric', *Journal of Archaeology and Ancient History*, XIV (2015), pp. 1–36

——, Fernando López-Sánchez and Helena Victor, 'The 5th Century Hoard of Theodosian Solidi from Stora Brunneby, Öland, Sweden: A Result from the Leo Project', *Fornvännen*, CVI/3 (2011), pp. 189–204

Fitzpatrick, Andrew P., *The Amesbury Archer and the Boscombe Bowmen: Bell Beaker Burials on Boscombe Down, Amesbury, Wiltshire* (Salisbury, 2011)

Fowler, Brenda, *Iceman: Uncovering the Life and Times of a Prehistoric Man Found in an Alpine Glacier* (New York, 2000)

Frei, Karin Margarita, et al., 'Tracing the Dynamic Life Story of a Bronze Age Female', *Scientific Reports* 5, article no. 10431

Gerritsen, Fokke, 'Domestic Times: Houses and Temporalities in Late Prehistoric Europe', in *Prehistoric Europe: Theory and Practice*, ed. A. Jones (Oxford, 2008), pp. 143–61

Geselowitz, Michael N., 'Technology and Social Change: Ironworking in the Rise of Social Complexity in Iron Age Central Europe', in *Tribe and Polity in Late Prehistoric Europe*, ed. D. B. Gibson and M. N. Geselowitz (New York, 1988), pp. 137–54

Gleeson, Dermot F., 'Discovery of Gold Gorget at Burren, Co. Clare', *Journal of the Royal Society of Antiquaries of Ireland*, IV/1 (1934), pp. 138–9

Goffart, Walter, *The Narrators of Barbarian History (AD 550–800): Jordanes, Gregory of Tours, Bede, and Paul the Deacon* (Princeton, NJ, 1988)

Goldhahn, Joakim, 'Bredarör on Kivik: A Monumental Cairn and the History of its Interpretation', *Antiquity*, LXXXIII/320 (2009), pp. 359–71

Goscinny, René, *René Goscinny raconte les secrets d'Astérix* (Paris, 2014)

Gregoratti, Leonardo, 'North Italic Settlers along the "Amber Route"', *Studia Antiqua et Archaeologica*, XIX/1 (2013), pp. 133–53

Halsall, Guy, 'Two Worlds Become One: A "Counter-intuitive" View of the Roman Empire and "Germanic" Migration', *German History*, XXXII/4 (2014), pp. 515–32

Hammond, Norman, 'Obituary: Glyn Edmund Daniel, 1914–1986', *American Antiquity*, LIV/2 (1989), pp. 234–9

Harding, Anthony, *European Societies in the Bronze Age* (Cambridge, 2000)

——, *Salt in Prehistoric Europe* (Leiden, 2013)

——, and Włodzimierz Rączkowski, 'Living on the Lake in the Iron Age: New Results from Aerial Photographs, Geophysical Survey and Dendrochronology on Sites of Biskupin Type', *Antiquity*, LXXXIV/324 (2010), pp. 386–404

Harl, Kenneth W., *Coinage in the Roman Economy, 300 BC to AD 700* (Baltimore, MD, 1996)

Hawkins, Gerald S., *Stonehenge Decoded* (Garden City, NY, 1965)

Heather, Peter J., *Empires and Barbarians: The Fall of Rome and the Birth of Europe* (New York, 2010)

Hughes, Susan S., et al., 'Anglo-Saxon Origins Investigated by Isotopic Analysis of Burials from Berinsfield, Oxfordshire, UK, *Journal of Archaeological Science*, XLII (2013), pp. 81–92

Ilkjær, Jørgen, *Illerup Ådal – Archaeology as a Magic Mirror* (Højbjerg, 2000)

Jażdżewska, Maria, 'A Roman Legionary Helmet Found in Poland', *Gladius*, 17 (1986), pp. 57–62

Jensen, Jørgen, 'The Hjortspring Boat Reconstructed', *Antiquity*, LXIII/240 (1989), pp. 531–5

Johnston, Susan A., 'Revisiting the Irish Royal Sites', *Emania*, XX (2006), pp. 53–9

——., Pam J. Crabtree and Douglas V. Campana, 'Performance, Place and Power at Dún Ailinne, a Ceremonial Site of the Irish Iron Age', *World Archaeology*, XLVI/2 (2014), pp. 206–23

Jones, Carleton, *The Burren and the Aran Islands* (Cork, 2004)

Jørgensen, Lars, 'Gudme-Lundeborg on Funen as a Model for Northern Europe?', in *The Gudme/Gudhem Phenomenon*, ed. O. Grimm and A. Pesch (Neumünster, 2011), pp. 77–89

——, Birger Storgaard and Lone Gebauer Thomsen, eds, *The Spoils of Victory: The North in the Shadow of the Roman Empire* (Copenhagen, 2003)

Kaul, Flemming, 'The Hjortspring Find: The Oldest of the Large Nordic War Booty Sacrifices', in *The Spoils of Victory: The North in the Shadow of the Roman Empire*, ed. L. Jørgensen, B. Storgaard and L. G. Thomsen (Copenhagen, 2003), pp. 212–23

Kelly, Eamonn P., 'An Archaeological Interpretation of Irish Iron Age Bog Bodies', in *The Archaeology of Violence: Interdisciplinary Approaches*, ed. S. Ralph (Albany, NY, 2013), pp. 232–40

Kern, Anton, et al., eds, *Kingdom of Salt: 7000 Years of Hallstatt* (Vienna, 2009)

Kostrzewski, Józef, 'Biskupin: An Early Iron Age Village in Western Poland', *Antiquity*, XII/47 (1938), pp. 311–17

Kristiansen, Kristian, 'Decentralized Complexity: The Case of Bronze Age Northern Europe', in *Pathways to Power: New Perspectives on the Emergence of Social Inequality*, ed. T. D. Price and G. M. Feinman (New York, 2010), pp. 169–92

Kulikowski, Michael, *Rome's Gothic Wars: From the Third Century to Alaric* (New York, 2007)

Larsson, Lars, 'The Iron Age Ritual Building at Uppåkra, Southern Sweden', *Antiquity*, LXXXI/311 (2007), pp. 11–25

——, 'The Skateholm Project: Late Mesolithic Coastal Settlement in Southern Sweden', in *Case Studies in European Prehistory*, ed. P. Bogucki (Boca Raton, FL, 1993), pp. 31–62

Larsson, Mikael, and Dominic Ingemark, 'Roman Horticulture beyond the Frontier: Garden Cultivation at Iron Age Uppåkra (Sweden)', *Journal of Roman Archaeology*, XXVIII (2015), pp. 393–402

Ling, Johan, 'War Canoes or Social Units? Human Representation in Rock-art Ships', *European Journal of Archaeology*, XV/3 (2012), pp. 465–85

——, and Joakim Goldhahn, 'Bronze Age Rock Art in Northern Europe: Contexts and Interpretations', in *The Oxford Handbook of the European Bronze Age*, ed. H. Fokkens and A. Harding (Oxford, 2013), pp. 270–90

Lobell, Jarrett A., and Samir S. Patel, 'Clovycavan and Old Croghan Men', *Archaeology*, LXIII/3 (2010)

Løvschal, Mette, and Mads Kähler Holst, 'Repeating Boundaries – Repertoires of Landscape Regulations in Southern Scandinavia in the Late Bronze Age and Pre-Roman Iron Age', *Danish Journal of Archaeology*, III/2 (2014), pp. 95–118

Maixner, Frank, et al., 'The 5300-year-old Helicobacter Pylori Genome of the Iceman', *Science*, CCCLI/6269 (2016), pp. 162–5

Megaw, John Vincent Stanley, 'The Vix Burial', *Antiquity*, XL/157 (1966), pp. 38–44

Menotti, Francesco, 'The Pfahlbauproblem and the History of Lake-dwelling Research in the Alps', *Oxford Journal of Archaeology*, XX/4 (2001), pp. 319–28

——, *Wetland Archaeology and Beyond: Theory and Practice* (Oxford, 2012)

Meyer, Caspar, *Greco-Scythian Art and the Birth of Eurasia: From Classical Antiquity to Russian Modernity* (Oxford, 2013)

Meyer, Christian, et al., 'The Massacre Mass Grave of Schöneck-Kilianstädten Reveals New Insights into Collective Violence in Early Neolithic Central Europe', *Proceedings of the National Academy of Sciences*, CXII/36 (2015), pp. 11217–22

Meyer, Michael, 'Roman Cultural Influence in Western Germania Magna', *The Oxford Handbook of the Archaeology of Roman Germany*, ed. S. James and S. Krmnicek (Oxford, 2015), DOI: 10.1093/oxfordhb/9780199665730.013.8 (forthcoming in print)

Midgley, Magdalena S., *The Megaliths of Northern Europe* (London, 2008)

Minnitt, Stephen, 'The Iron Age Wetlands of Central Somerset', in *Somerset Archaeology: Papers to Mark 150 Years of the Somerset Archaeological and Natural History Society*, ed. C. J. Webster (Taunton, 2001), pp. 73–8

Mohen, Jean-Pierre, and Gérard Bailloud, *La Vie quotidienne: Les Fouilles du Fort-Harrouard* (Paris, 1987)

Morse, Michael, *How the Celts Came to Britain* (Stroud, 2005)

Mühlenbrock, Josef, and Mike Schweissing, '"Frisch Erforscht!": Die Skelette aus dem römischen Töpferofen in Haltern am See', *Archäologie in Westfalen-Lippe 2009* (2010), pp. 261–5

Musolff, Andreas, 'From Teamchef Arminius to Hermann Junior: Glocalised Discourses about a National Foundation Myth', *Language and Intercultural Communication*, XII/1 (2012), pp. 24–36

Needham, Stuart, Andrew J. Lawson and Ann Woodward, '"A Noble Group of Barrows": Bush Barrow and the Normanton Down Early Bronze Age Cemetery Two Centuries On', *The Antiquaries Journal*, 90 (2010), pp. 1–39

Nielsen, Poul Otto, Klavs Randsborg and Henrik Thrane, eds, *The Archaeology of Gudme and Lundeborg* (Copenhagen, 1994)

Noort, Robert Van de, 'Seafaring and Riverine Navigation in the Bronze Age of Europe', in *The Oxford Handbook of the European Bronze Age*, ed. A. Harding and H. Fokkens (Oxford, 2013), pp. 382–97

O'Brien, William, *Iverni: A Prehistory of Cork* (Cork, 2012)

——, *Prehistoric Copper Mining in Europe, 5500–500 BC* (Oxford, 2014)

Oeggl, Klaus, et al., 'The Reconstruction of the Last Itinerary of Ötzi, the Neolithic Iceman, by Pollen Analyses from Sequentially Sampled Gut Extracts', *Quaternary Science Reviews*, XXVI/7 (2007), pp. 853–61

Pásztor, Emília, 'Nebra Disk', in *Handbook of Archaeoastronomy and Ethnoastronomy*, ed. C.L.N. Ruggles (New York, 2015), pp. 1349–56

Pearson, Mike Parker, et al., 'Stonehenge', in *The Oxford Handbook of the European Bronze Age*, ed. H. Fokkens and A. Harding (Oxford, 2013), pp. 159–78

Pernter, Patrizia, et al., 'Radiologic Proof for the Iceman's Cause of Death (ca. 5300 BP)', *Journal of Archaeological Science*, XXXIV/11 (2007), pp. 1784–86

Picaud, Carine, ed., *Astérix de A à Z* (Paris, 2013)

Piggott, Stuart, *Ancient Europe, from the Beginnings of Agriculture to Classical Antiquity: A Survey* (Edinburgh, 1965)

Piotrovsky, Boris, 'Excavations and Discoveries in Scythian Lands', *Metropolitan Museum of Art Bulletin*, XXXII/5 (1973), pp. 26–31

Piotrowski, Wojciech, 'The Importance of the Biskupin Wet Site for Twentieth-century Polish Archaeology', in *Hidden Dimensions: The Cultural Significance of Wetland Archaeology*, ed. K. Bernick (Vancouver, 1998), pp. 89–106

Plicht, J. van der, et al., 'Dating Bog Bodies by Means of 14C-AMS', *Journal of Archaeological Science*, XXXI/4 (2004), pp. 471–91

Plunkett, Gill, et al., 'A Multi-Proxy Palaeoenvironmental Investigation of the Findspot of an Iron Age Bog Body from Oldcroghan, Co. Offaly, Ireland', *Journal of Archaeological Science*, XXXVI/2 (2009), pp. 265–77

Price, T. Douglas, *Ancient Scandinavia: An Archaeological History from the First Humans to the Vikings* (New York, 2015)

Pryor, Francis, *Flag Fen: Life and Death of a Prehistoric Landscape* (Stroud, 2005)

Raftery, Barry, 'Ancient Trackways in Corlea Bog, Co. Longford', *Archaeology Ireland*, I/2 (1987), pp. 60–64

Randsborg, Klavs, 'Beyond the Roman Empire: Archaeological Discoveries in Gudme on Funen, Denmark', *Oxford Journal of Archaeology*, IX/3 (1990), pp. 355–66

——, *Hjortspring: Warfare and Sacrifice in Early Europe* (Aarhus, 1995)

Rasbach, Gabi, 'Waldgirmes', *Archaeological Journal*, 170, supp. 1 (2013), pp. 18–21

Reitsema, Laurie J., and Tomasz Kozłowski, 'Diet and Society in Poland before the State: Stable Isotope Evidence from a Wielbark Population (2nd c. AD)', *Anthropological Review*, LXXVI/1 (2013), pp. 1–22

Rieck, Flemming, 'The Ships from Nydam Bog', in *The Spoils of Victory, the North in the Shadow of the Roman Empire*, ed. L. Jørgensen, B. Storgaard and L. G. Thomsen (Copenhagen, 2003), pp. 296–309

Rolle, Renate, 'Scythians: Between Mobility, Tomb Architecture and Early Urban Structures', in *The Barbarians of Ancient Europe: Realities and*

Interactions, ed. L. Bonfante (Cambridge, 2011), pp. 107–31

——, *The World of the Scythians* (Berkeley, CA, 1989)

Rowley-Conwy, Peter, *From Genesis to Prehistory: The Archaeological Three Age System and its Contested Reception in Denmark, Britain, and Ireland* (Oxford, 2007)

Roymans, Nico, *Ethnic Identity and Imperial Power: The Batavians in the Early Roman Empire* (Amsterdam, 2004)

Ruffing, Kai, 'Friedliche Beziehungen. Der Handel zwischen den römischen Provinzen und Germanien', in *Feindliche Nachbarn: Rom und die Germanen*, ed. H. Schneider (Cologne, 2008), pp. 153–65

Ruggles, Clive L. N., 'Stonehenge and its Landscape', in *Handbook of Archaeoastronomy and Ethnoastronomy*, ed. C.L.N. Ruggles (New York, 2015), pp. 1223–38

Sanden, Wijnand A. B. van der, 'Bog Bodies: Underwater Burials, Sacrifices and Executions', in *The Oxford Handbook of Wetland Archaeology*, ed. F. Menotti (Oxford, 2013), pp. 401–16

Scarre, Chris, *Exploring Prehistoric Europe* (New York, 1998)

——, *Landscapes of Neolithic Brittany* (Oxford, 2011)

Schibler, Jörg, Stephanie Jacomet and Alice Choyke, 'Arbon-Bleiche 3', in *Ancient Europe, 8000 BC–AD 1000: An Encyclopedia of the Barbarian World*, ed. P. Bogucki and P. J. Crabtree, vol. I (New York, 2004), pp. 395–7

Schier, Wolfram, 'Central and Eastern Europe', in *The Oxford Handbook of Neolithic Europe*, ed. C. Fowler, J. Harding and D. Hofmann (Oxford, 2015), pp. 99–120

Schnurbein, S. von, 'Augustus in Germania and His New "Town" at Waldgirmes East of the Rhine', *Journal of Roman Archaeology*, XVI (2003), pp. 93–107

Sharples, Niall M., *English Heritage Book of Maiden Castle* (London, 1991)

Shennan, Stephen, 'Cost, Benefit and Value in the Organization of Early European Copper Production', *Antiquity*, LXXIII/280 (1999), pp. 352–63

Shetelig, Haakon, and Fredrik Johannessen, *Das Nydamschiff* (Copenhagen, 1930)

Standish, Christopher D., et al., 'A Non-Local Source of Irish Chalcolithic and Early Bronze Age Gold', *Proceedings of the Prehistoric Society*, LXXXI (2015), pp. 149–77

Steinel, Monika, 'Archaeology, National Socialism, and Rehabilitation: The Case of Herbert Jahnkuhn (1905–1990)', in *Ethics and the Archaeology of Violence*, ed. A. González-Ruibal and G. Moshenska (New York, 2015), pp. 153–65

Stout, Geraldine, *Newgrange and the Bend of the Boyne* (Cork, 2002)

——, and Matthew Stout, *Newgrange* (Cork, 2008)

Taylor, Timothy, 'The Gundestrup Cauldron', *Scientific American*, CCLXVI (1992), pp. 84–9

Thomas, Mark G., Michael P. H. Stumpf and Heinrich Härke, 'Evidence for an Apartheid-like Social Structure in Early Anglo-Saxon England',

Proceedings of the Royal Society of London B: Biological Sciences,
CCLXXIII/1601 (2006), pp. 2651–7

Urbańczyk, Przemysław, 'The Goths in Poland – Where Did They Come from
and When Did They Leave?', *European Journal of Archaeology*, I/3 (1998),
pp. 397–415

Urbanus, Jason, 'Eternal Banquets of the Early Celts', *Archaeology*, LXVIII/6
(2015), pp. 44–9

——, 'Fire in the Fens', *Archaeology*, LXX/1 (2017), pp. 34–9.

Vedeler, Marianne, and Lise Bender Jørgensen, 'Out of the Norwegian Glaciers:
Lendbreen – a Tunic from the Early First Millennium AD', *Antiquity*,
LXXXVII/337 (2013), pp. 788–801

Wells, Colin, 'What's New along the Lippe: Recent Work in North Germany',
Britannia, XXIX (1998), pp. 457–64

Wells, Peter S., *The Barbarians Speak: How the Conquered Peoples Shaped
Roman Europe* (Princeton, NJ, 1999)

——, *The Battle that Stopped Rome: Emperor Augustus, Arminius, and the
Slaughter of the Legions in the Teutoburg Forest* (New York, 2003)

——, 'Investigating the Origins of Temperate Europe's First Towns: Excavations
at Hascherkeller, 1978–1981', in *Case Studies in European Prehistory*,
ed. P. Bogucki (Boca Raton, FL, 1993), pp. 181–203

——, 'Kelheim', in *Ancient Europe, 8000 BC–AD 1000: An Encyclopedia of the
Barbarian World*, ed. P. Bogucki and P. J. Crabtree, vol. II (New York,
2004), pp. 247–9

——, *Settlement, Economy, and Cultural Change at the End of the European Iron
Age: Excavations at Kelheim in Bavaria, 1987–1991* (Ann Arbor, MI, 1993)

West, Stanley, *West Stow: The Anglo-Saxon Village* (Ipswich, 1985)

Westerdahl, Christer, 'Boats Apart: Building and Equipping an Iron-Age and
Early-Medieval Ship in Northern Europe', *International Journal of Nautical
Archaeology*, XXXVII/1 (2008), pp. 17–31

Young, Bailey, 'Tomb of Childeric', in *Ancient Europe, 8000 BC–AD 1000:
An Encyclopedia of the Barbarian World*, ed. P. Bogucki and P. J. Crabtree,
vol. II (New York, 2004), pp. 519–24

ACKNOWLEDGEMENTS

Ben Hayes of Reaktion Books motivated me to write this book, and I am very grateful for his encouragement and prodding. Over 25 years ago, Paul Bahn encouraged me to break out from my narrow interests in early European farmers in Poland and write short pieces for a general audience. The cumulative results of these efforts helped shape the discussion of many sites and finds described in this book. For over thirty years, Pam Crabtree has been an esteemed colleague who has kept me up to date on discoveries in the later prehistory of western Europe. Our collaboration on *Ancient Europe, 8000 BC–AD 1000: An Encyclopedia of the Barbarian World* (New York, 2004) and our teaching together at Princeton in the late 1980s enabled me to obtain a broad overview of the Bronze Age and Iron Age societies outside my own research interests. Vince Poor, as dean of the School of Engineering and Applied Science at Princeton University, where I work, encouraged my participation in archaeological scholarship and supported my attendance at conferences. Traci Miller, through meticulous attention to the demands of our office, enabled me to divert my attention occasionally from my deanly responsibilities to write and think. Our student assistants Erin O'Hearn and Alev Baysoy helped compile lists of sites, check references and mark editorial queries. It has been a pleasure to work with cartographer Sebastian Ballard on the preparation of the maps. Amy Salter and Jess Chandler saw the book through the editorial process with exacting attention to detail. Finally, I must acknowledge the support of my family: my wife Virginia and daughters Caroline and Marianna, who have accompanied me on visits to many sites mentioned in this book. In fact, the proposal for this book was drafted in a hotel room in Washington, DC, while Caroline was downstairs with Marianna and Ginny getting ready for her wedding to C. J. Cross later that afternoon. Little did they know that, upstairs, *The Barbarians* were astir!

PHOTO ACKNOWLEDGEMENTS

The author and publishers wish to express their thanks to the below sources of illustrative material and/or permission to reproduce it. Some locations of artworks are also given below.

Søren H. Anderson: p. 30; Muzeum Archeologiczne, Poznań, p. 92; © Sebastian Ballard: pp. 23, 24; Bibliothèque nationale de France: p. 185; © BOAT 1550 BC project: p. 67; Peter Bogucki: pp. 16, 51 (after drawing by Irene Deluis), 169 (after Larsson), 194; photo © Denis Gliksman, INRAP, used by permission: pp. 108–9; Kalmar County Museum: p. 186; image courtesy of Seweryn Rzepecki, University of Łódź: p. 161; The Metropolitan Museum of Art, New York: p. 10; National Museum, Copenhagen: pp. 19, 62–3, 73, 74, 165; National Museum, Dublin: p. 85; National Portrait Gallery, London: p. 197; Norfolk Museum: p. 77; © P. Pétrequin, Centre de la Recherches Archeologique de la Vallée de l'Ain, used by permission: p. 34; © South Tyrol Museum of Archaeology, Bolzano, www.iceman.it, used by permission: pp. 39, 42; image © Tiroler-Kräuterdestillerie, used by permission: p. 212; Marianne Vedeler: p. 214.

Kevin King, the copyright holder of the image on p. 122, Carole Raddato, the copyright holder of the image on p. 146, Xuan Che, the copyright holder of the image on p. 106, and N Stjerna, the copyright holder of the image on p.70, have published these online under conditions imposed by a Creative Commons CC-BY-SA 2.0 license; Rama, the copyright holder of the image on p. 33, has published online under conditions imposed by a Creative Commons CC-BY-SA 2.0 FR license; Ash_Crow, the copyright holder of the image on p. 184, Erlend Bjørtvedt, the copyright holder of the image on pp. 80–81, Bullenwächter, the copyright holder of the image on p. 125, Cherubino, the copyright holder of the image on p. 142, Dbachmann, the copyright holder of the image on p. 65, Eric Gaba, the copyright holder of the image on p. 139, Jochen Jahnke, the copyright holder of the image on p. 135, LepoRello, the copyright holder of the image on pp. 208–9, Ludek, the copyright holder of the image on p. 95, Gun Powder Ma, the copyright holder of the image on p. 116, Midnightblueowl, the copyright holder of the image on pp. 118–19, Nationalmuseet, the copyright holder of the image

Page numbers in *italic* refer to illustrations